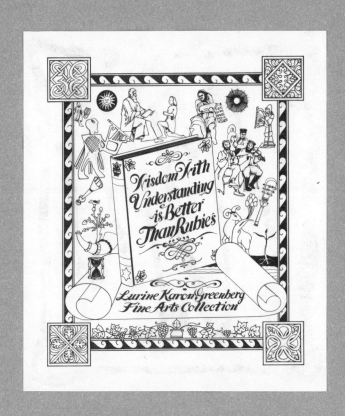

THE UNICORN TAPESTRIES

THE UNICORN TAPESTRIES

at The Metropolitan Museum of Art

Adolfo Salvatore Cavallo

The Metropolitan Museum of Art, New York
Harry N. Abrams, Inc., Publishers

Published by The Metropolitan Museum of Art, New York

John P. O'Neill, Editor in Chief
Barbara Burn, Project Editor
Tsang Seymour Design, Designer
Katherine van Kessel, Production Manager

Library of Congress Cataloging-in-Publication Data

Cavallo, Adolph S.
The unicorn tapestries in the Metropolitan Museum of Art /
Adolfo Salvatore Cavallo.
    p. cm.
Includes bibliographical references.
ISBN 0-87099-868-4 (MMA hc). – ISBN 0-87099-869-2
(MMA pbk.: alk. paper) – ISBN 0-8109-3947-9 (Abrams hc)
1. Hunt of the unicorn (Tapestries) 2. Tapestry, Gothic–France.
3. Art and mythology. 4. Unicorns in art. 5. Christian art
and symbolism–Medieval, 5001500–Themes, motives.
6. Cloisters (Museum) I. Metropolitan Museum of Art
(New York, N.Y.) II. Title.
NK3049.U538 1998
746.3944–dc21   98.4153

Appendix 1, "Flora in the Unicorn Tapestries," was originally published as two articles in the *Journal of The New York
Botanical Garden* in May and June 1941 and later appeared as
a booklet in 1947. Copyright (c) 1941, 1947 by The New York
Botanical Garden. Reprinted with permission.

Appendix 2, "Fauna in the Unicorn Tapestries," was origi-
nally published as Chapter 3 in Margaret B. Freeman's book
The Unicorn Tapestries, published in 1976 by The
Metropolitan Museum of Art. Copyright (c) 1976 by The
Metropolitan Museum of Art

The photographs in this book, unless otherwise credited,
were taken by Bruce Schwarz of The Photograph Studio,
The Metropolitan Museum of Art.
Figures 69–74 © Photos RMN–R.G. Ojeda

Frontispiece: Detail from *The Unicorn is Found* from *The
Hunt of the Unicorn as an Allegory of the Passion*. Southern
Netherlands, 1495—1505. The Metropolitan Museum of Art,
Gift of John D. Rockefeller Jr., 1937 (37.80.2)

Composition by Tsang Seymour Design
Printed and bound by Julio Soto, Madrid, Spain

Harry N. Abrams, Inc.
100 Fifth Avenue
New York, N.Y. 10011
www.abramsbooks.com

Contents

Foreword

One of the most popular attractions at The Cloisters, which houses part of the Metropolitan Museum's splendid collection of medieval European art, is a series of tapestries depicting the hunt of the fabled unicorn. Visitors from all over the world have traveled to The Cloisters, some of them specifically to view these magnificent works of art, which were made in one of the major tapestry-weaving centers in the southern Netherlands, such as Brussels, between the years 1495 and 1505. Most tapestries were woven in sets in order to tell a story, honor the individual or family who commissioned them, or celebrate an event—in some cases all three. While many tapestries that have survived from the late Middle Ages illustrate the high quality these works often exemplified, the unicorn tapestries that are the subject of this book are among the few that can be considered of the first rank. They are imaginatively conceived, beautifully designed, and exceptionally well made. Perhaps most important, however, is the fact that the images captured here in silk, wool, and metal yarns are superbly memorable. From the vulnerable unicorn to the hunters—each of them individually portrayed—to the naturalistically depicted flora and fauna of the landscape: all these are subjects that move us, that remain in our memory long after we have viewed them.

One of the most intriguing aspects of these tapestries is the mystery that surrounds them. For whom were they made? What stories do they tell? Adolfo Cavallo, the author of this book and a distinguished scholar who has previously catalogued the Museum's collection of medieval tapestries, addresses these issues and others in the pages that follow. However, even he recognizes that some of the answers may never be known, so the mystery continues.

To complement the author's discussion of the unicorn itself as a secular and Christian symbol, we have included two previously published essays on the flora and fauna for which the tapestries are also famous.

We hope that this book, the first in twenty-two years to be devoted to the unicorn tapestries, will enhance the viewer's experience of these sublime works of art and provide those who have never had the opportunity to see them with a sense of their splendor and an insight into the reasons they are among the most beloved masterpieces in the Metropolitan Museum's collection.

Philippe de Montebello
Director, The Metropolitan Museum of Art

Opposite: The Unicorn Is Found, *detail of Figure 34*

Tales of the Unicorn
A New Look
at the Unicorn Tapestries

ADOLFO SALVATORE CAVALLO

The *Hunt of the Unicorn* tapestries, like all extraordinarily beautiful and enigmatic works of art, have excited the admiration and curiosity of scholars ever since they were first mentioned in the literature in 1888. A tapestry expert, Xavier Barbier de Montault, brought the unicorn tapestries to public attention that year in an article he wrote about a six-piece set called *The Lady with the Unicorn* (*La Dame à Licorne*), which is now one of the jewels of the Musée de Cluny in Paris (see Figures 69–74). In his article Barbier de Montault reminisced about a visit he had made eight years earlier to the château de Verteuil, the country seat of the de La Rochefoucauld family a few kilometers north of Angoulême, where he had first seen the *Hunt of the Unicorn* tapestries now in the collection of The Metropolitan Museum of Art. From 1888 onward, these hangings have been examined, interpreted, and discussed at great length in both scientific and popular literature, perhaps at greater length than any other late-medieval tapestries except *The Lady with the Unicorn*.

These two sets of tapestries contain mysteries, so it is not surprising that both have been encumbered with myths and legends concerning their meaning and their pedigrees. A number of publications concerning the hunting tapestries were issued by The Cloisters and The Metropolitan Museum of Art between 1938 (when they were first shown to the public on the occasion of the opening of The Cloisters, the Museum's medieval branch located in upper Manhattan) and 1993, when a complete catalogue of the Museum's collection of medieval tapestries was published. In that span of fifty-five years, many specialists offered interpretations of the subject matter and theories about the origin of the hangings. What do the images mean? For whom were these tapestries woven? Who designed them and where were they made?

The present publication attempts to explain the tapestries in the light of the most recent research. Inevitably, the ideas offered here differ in many respects from the theories and statements published earlier, as a number of new facts and interpretations have been put forward in

Figure 1. The Unicorn Leaps out of the Stream, *detail of Figure 39*

the years since 1938. This introductory essay is offered as a means of separating old ideas from new and fact from legend before we embark on our new look at the tapestries themselves.

James J. Rorimer, who as curator of medieval art obtained *The Hunt of the Unicorn* for the Museum and wrote the first monograph on the set in 1938, endorsed the idea that the tapestries deal with the subject of the Incarnation (with the unicorn as a symbol of Christ). He acknowledged, however, that the designer had emphasized the secular appeal of the hunt over the religious content and pointed out that the piece showing the unicorn chained to a tree in a fenced garden (see Figure 23) represents not only the Incarnation but also, because of the golden chain (a symbol of marriage) and the pomegranates (a symbol of fertility) growing on the tree, the consummation of marriage.

Rorimer's interpretation led to the idea that the tapestries were woven to celebrate a marriage, and this seemed to be supported by a traditional belief in the de La Rochefoucauld family that the tapestries were woven for Jean II de La Rochefoucauld and Marguerite de Barbezieux, who were married in 1450. The style of the compositions indicates a later date, however, so Rorimer and other scholars determined that this could not have been the marriage in question. In a later article, published in the Museum's *Bulletin* in 1942, Rorimer proposed that the marriage celebrated by *The Hunt of the Unicorn* was that of Anne of Brittany and King Louis XII of France, which took place on January 8, 1499, a date that fits in perfectly with the style of the tapestries. However, in a revised edition of the Cloisters monograph (1945), he suggested that the tapestry showing the unicorn chained to the pomegranate tree and the one showing the start of the hunt (see Figure 16) were added to the other pieces some years after 1499, in celebration of the marriage in 1514 of Anne of Brittany's daughter Claude to François I, king of France.

A great deal of evidence that was regarded as valid in 1942 was marshaled to support the Anne and Louis theory. The lord and lady who stand in the right foreground of the tapestry showing the dead unicorn brought to the castle (Figure 2) are portraits of Anne and Louis. The cipher AE (the E reversed) refers to Anne: these are the first and last letters of her given name, and the cord tying the letters together is the cordelière of the Franciscan order to which Anne was dedicated. After her marriage to Louis, Anne's livery color of white appears along with his own red and yellow in some of the costumes represented in the tapestries. There are three fleurs-de-lis (the lilies in the royal arms of France) on two of the hunting dogs' collars in one of the tapestries (Figure 39). Another dog's collar shows the letters OFANCRE, which are an abbreviation of OF[R]ANC[ORUM]RE[X], a salute to the king of the French (see Figure 46), and some of the banners flying from castle towers show Louis's heraldic porcupine and Anne's cross. The royal arms of both Anne and Louis once decorated the sky areas in most of the tapestries, but they were apparently cut away during the Revolution to save the tapestries from destruction by the mobs that looted the château de Verteuil in 1793 during the Reign of Terror.

In a more ambitious and detailed monograph written by Margaret B. Freeman and published by the Museum in 1976, each of these claims was reexamined and discarded as being invalid in the light of subsequent research. Freeman suggested that the tapestries showing the chained unicorn and the start of the hunt were not woven later than the other pieces but were either designed by a different artist or woven by less competent weavers. Furthermore, she speculated that these two pieces may have been made as a cover, headcloth, or ceiling for a bed in a room where the other unicorn tapestries decorated the walls. The AE cipher remains a mystery. Does it represent the initials of two given names (those of a husband and wife) or the initials of the given and family names of a single person or the initial letters of a secret motto or the first and last letters of a single given name? The cipher FR appears once in this group of hangings, applied to the modern sky fabric in the piece showing the unicorn leaping out of the water (see Figure 39); the cipher may represent François I de La Rochefoucauld, who lived during the time the tapestries were woven. Freeman noted that the cipher is not part of the original fabric of these wall hangings but suggested that it might have been woven on a smaller scale to decorate the valances of a tapestry bed.

The catalogue raisonné of medieval tapestries in the Museum's collection, written by myself and published in 1993, accepts much of the material published in 1976 and incorporates a number of newer ideas developed both here and in France. The *Hunt of the Unicorn* and the *Lady with the Unicorn* sets were exhibited together in Paris in the winter of 1973–74. On that occasion and in the years that followed, French scholars suggested that the seven hunting tapestries represent three different but related sets of hangings. Specialists here and abroad have also dismissed the idea that the pieces showing the start of the hunt and the chained unicorn were made as bed furnishings. Both pieces are 12 feet, 1 inch (3.68 meters) in height, which is too tall for a headcloth and too long for a bed ceiling or bed cover. The start of the hunt is 10 feet, 4 inches (3.15 meters) wide and the chained unicorn is 8 feet, 3 inches wide (2.52 meters), both so wide that it seems unlikely either piece would have served as the headcloth or ceiling of a bed. In the 1993 catalogue I also rejected the idea that the FR cipher was part of the hunting tapestries, and I agreed that the AE remains a mystery.

There is, however, no mystery about the date of the tapestries. Certain details of the men's and women's costumes—the shape of the men's round-toed shoes, doublets, and hose, as well as their hair styles, and the snug bodices and high-hipped skirts of the women's gowns, as well as the form of their headdresses—all point to the years around 1495 to 1505. The style of the drawing and composition suggest the same period.

In the pages that follow, I do not stray far from the comments made in my catalogue, but I have added and altered a few details. As more research is conducted in the years ahead, and as new minds are brought to bear on the questions that have not yet been satisfactorily answered concerning this remarkable group of tapestries, I expect that much of what follows here will change also.

History of the Tapestries

The seven *Hunt of the Unicorn* tapestries in the Metropolitan Museum's collection can be traced back to 1680 through documents and viewers' reports. In March of that year an inventory was taken of the property belonging to the recently deceased François VI de La Rochefoucauld in his Paris town house. That inventory lists, in the Great Chamber, "hangings of *haute lisse* tapestry representing a unicorn hunt in seven pieces containing twenty-two aulnes in length by four aulnes in height, or thereabouts, appraised at the amount of 1,500 livres." (The term *haute lisse*, which in the seventeenth century did not necessarily mean, as it does now, that the tapestries were woven on a vertical loom, will be discussed in the chapter that deals with the manufacture of the tapestries, page 79.) These dimensions work out in modern terms to approximately 86 feet, 7½ inches (26.40 meters) by 15 feet 9 inches (4.80 meters), which refers to the combined width of all seven pieces and the height of each.

At some time between 1680 and 1728 the seven tapestries were moved to the family's château in Verteuil. They were inventoried there in 1728 following the death of François VIII de La Rochefoucauld. Five pieces, again described as *haute lisse* tapestries, were hanging in "the large bedroom of the new building," and it was noted that they were almost half worn out. Two other pieces, cited as having holes in many places, were in a furniture storeroom. Their poor condition probably accounts for their having been separated from the others, and it also explains why these two hangings were appraised at 45 livres while the other five were assigned a value of 150 livres.

The seven hangings managed to escape destruction at the time of the Reign of Terror in 1793–94, that horrific period during the French Revolution when works of art containing symbols of royalty and the aristocracy were subject to destruction. The

Figure 2. The Unicorn Is Killed and Brought to the Castle, *detail of Figure 50 showing the lord and lady of the castle*

Figure 3. The Unicorn Is Killed, *detail of Figure 50 showing the castle of the host of the hunt*

overseeing committee in the nearby town of Ruffec, which represented the central government authority of the Committee of Public Safety, instructed the corresponding authority in Verteuil to "Examine these old tapestries. Respect them because they show no signs of royalty; they contain stories." The populist mobs who looted the château de Verteuil in 1793, therefore, simply took the tapestries as they were, along with other property belonging to the de La Rochefoucauld family.

The tapestries remained out of sight for another two generations. People in the neighborhood claimed that the hangings were being used to cover espaliered trees and to protect potatoes stored in barns from freezing. It may have been during this period of neglect that the tapestries lost approximately 3 feet, 8 inches (1.12 meters) of their height and 15 feet, 11 inches (4.79 meters) of their combined width, which includes most of the fabric of the one piece representing *The Mystic Hunt of the Unicorn*. Only two fragments of that tapestry have survived (see Figure 27). We can

therefore calculate that the other six pieces have lost about 5 feet, 2½ inches (2.37 meters) in the aggregate from their sides.

All of the hangings show relatively little restoration. What was missing has been rewoven or replaced. The most significant losses are these: the sky areas of the four hangings in the Passion group, which have been replaced with modern fabric imitating tapestry weave and dyed in tones of blue; the entire lowest portion of *The Start of the Hunt*, which has been rewoven with a pattern imitating the rest of the millefleurs ground; and the lower right corner of *The Unicorn Is Killed*, which has been replaced

with pieces of a later tapestry. Millefleurs tapestries, woven in great quantities between about 1400 and 1550, were characterized by a flat, usually green-colored background studded with many varieties of blooming plants, floral sprigs, or flowering stalks, against which were set figures, animals, trees, heraldic motifs, and other kinds of objects.

In the early 1850s, the comte Hippolyte de La Rochefoucauld and the comtesse

Figure 4. Photograph of the tapestries at the château de Verteuil, about 1890–1900

Figure 5. View of The Cloisters, Fort Tryon Park, New York, where
the unicorn tapestries are on permanent display

Elisabeth embarked on a program of recovering the property that had been looted from the château of Verteuil during the Revolution. So, when a peasant's wife approached with news that her husband had some "old curtains" covering vegetables in their barn, the comte and comtesse bought them. The old curtains were, in fact, the lost *Hunt of the Unicorn* tapestries. By 1856 they had been restored and were hanging in a salon of the château at Verteuil. The prolific nineteenth-century tapestry historian Xavier Barbier de Montault saw the hangings there in 1880 and mentioned them in the account he wrote in 1888 of the *Lady with the Unicorn* tapestries now in Paris (see Figures 69–74). He said that the La Rochefoucauld tapestries were somewhat restored but looking fresh, that one of them had suffered losses, and that one of its two fragments had been made into a portiere.

In 1905, when Émile Biais saw *The Hunt of the Unicorn* at Verteuil, he noted that the colors in the six tapestries were astonishingly bright despite the great age of the hangings, but he made no reference to a seventh piece or to any fragments. Louis Serbat, writing in 1913 about works of art in the château de Verteuil, again mentioned only six of the hangings and ranked them among the most beautiful unicorn tapestries in the world. In a book he published about the same time, the tapestry specialist Jules Guiffrey wrote that he had seen six unicorn tapestries in one of the salons of the château de Verteuil.

It was some years later, in 1922, that Comte Aimery de La Rochefoucauld, then chatelain of Verteuil, allowed the Parisian art dealer Édouard Larcade to exhibit the six tapestries under his auspices at the Anderson Galleries in New York. John D. Rockefeller Jr. saw the tapestries there and bought them. He had them installed in a specially designed room in his residence on Fifty-fourth Street, where they hung from 1923 until 1937, when they were transferred to a gallery expressly designed for them in the new Cloisters branch of the Metropolitan Museum in Fort Tryon Park.

The seventh tapestry, which survived only in the form of the two fragments of weaving from the upper left quarter of the original hanging, came to The Cloisters by a different route. In 1936 William H. Forsyth, a curator in the Museum's Department of Medieval Art who was engaged in special research on *The Hunt of the Unicorn*, visited Aimery's son Gabriel de La Rochefoucauld in Paris and learned that the family still had the two fragments. The Museum arranged to buy them and to have them installed in The Cloisters with the other six hangings when the new museum in Fort Tryon Park opened to the public in 1938.

The Unicorn
What It Was and When It Thrived

The idea of a quadruped with a single horn growing from the center of its forehead is an ancient one. Sculptured figures of such beasts have survived from as early as the eighth century B.C., but the first verbal account appears early in the fourth century B.C. in a book about India written by a Greek physician named Ctesias, who had practiced medicine for a time at the court of the Persian king Artaxerxes II. Ctesias had never been to India, but he nevertheless described, on the basis of tales told by travelers, a wild donkey the size of a horse that had a single horn growing on its forehead between the eyes. Its body was apparently white, its head purple, and its eyes dark blue. The horn was parti-colored, white at the base, crimson at the tip, and black between. Ctesias reported that anyone who drank out of the horn would be immune to poisons and would not suffer from convulsions. It is likely that this animal was in fact the Indian rhinoceros, with various fanciful embellishments. The Indian rhinoceros is the only actual one-

horned animal, and some Asians have believed in the pharmaceutical power of rhino horn for centuries, paying high prices for it even to this day.

Aristotle, writing in his history of animals some fifty years later, dismissed Ctesias's description of the one-horned creature as pure fantasy but did not doubt that something like it existed. He knew of two one-horned animals: the oryx, with a cloven hoof (in actuality a wild African antelope with two horns), and an Indian ass whose foot was solid, like that of a horse (in actuality an onager, which has no horns at all, or perhaps a version of Ctesias's rhinoceros).

The unicorn continued its mythical evolution through the Roman Empire. Julius Caesar wrote in his account of the conquest of Gaul in the mid–first century A.D. that unicorns and other creatures no man had ever seen were living in the unexplored

Figure 6. The Unicorn in Captivity, detail of Figure 23.

outer reaches of the great forest in south-western Germany. The naturalist Pliny the Elder (A.D. 23–79), who ridiculed Pegasus, sirens, and other mythological beasts, nevertheless claimed, as Ctesias had done, that there lived in India a single-horned beast, the *monoceros*. Pliny's unicorn had a stag's head with a single black horn, the body of a horse, feet like an elephant's, and a boar's tail—again most likely a rhinoceros. Another Roman naturalist, Aelian (ca. A.D. 170–ca. 235), accepted Ctesias's unicorn as a creature that lived in the remote mountains of India, as large as a horse and

Figure 7. Painting of a narwhal by Richard Ellis (Photo Researchers)

as swift as the wind. It had red body hair and mane, feet like an elephant's, a tail like a goat's, and a single black horn. This animal, too, was probably a version of the rhinoceros. However, Aelian added a significant detail: his creature's horn had a natural spiral pattern. This raises the question whether the tusks of the Arctic narwhal, which are not black but markedly spiraled, unlike the horn of a rhinoceros or the ringed horn of the wild goat-antelope, could have been known at that early date and already adopted as the "proper" horn for a unicorn.

Contradictory and inaccurate as these early accounts may be, they agreed on two critical points. First, the unicorn was so swift and fierce that no beast or man could capture it. Second, the creature's horn possessed miraculous medicinal power, and anyone who drank from it would be protected from harm by disease or poison. Although the rhinoceros horn had for centuries been a valuable commodity in the Far East for this reason, a lucrative trade began to develop during the twelfth century in Europe, not of rhino horn but of what was in fact the extended upper left tooth of the male narwhal, a small Arctic whale (Figure 7). Narwhal tusks, identified and sold as unicorn horns, continued to be valued in parts of Europe through the eighteenth century. These tusks were often collected whole; Queen Elizabeth I inherited one and was given another in 1577 by Martin Frobisher, the British captain, who had seen a "sea unicorn" on his voyage to the Arctic. Narwhal tusks were also cut up and used in the construction of drinking and eating utensils, or, in fragments, as proving pieces to dip into suspect liquids. Frederick III, king of Denmark and Norway in the mid-seventeenth century, had a throne made with the material. Scrapings from the "horn" were also put in water and drunk as medicine until the middle of the eighteenth century, although apothecaries in urban parts of Europe no longer believed in the efficacy of unicorn therapy.

So far we have been dealing with "scientific" accounts of the unicorn's existence, but the spiritual life of this fabulous creature also has a history that extends far before the birth of Christ, with whom the unicorn eventually became identified. That history, interestingly, is based on what is likely to have been an error in translation from the Hebrew to the Greek, which took place in the third to second century B.C., when a group of scholars known as the Seventy produced a Greek version of the Old Testament, later called the Septuagint. In Deuteronomy 33:17, Joseph is referred to in the original Hebrew as a first born ox in his majesty. The Book of Job (39:9–10) asks whether the strength of the wild ox can be harnessed with ropes and whether it will follow you to harrow the furrows. The word in Hebrew for this "ox" is *re'em*, which subsequent scholars have identified as an urus—a large and fierce species of wild ox, the ancestor of our domestic cattle. At the time the Greek scholars were working on the Septuagint, however, the urus was extinct in all but the northern forests of Europe, and they could find no suitable translation for the word *re'em*. For some reason, perhaps influenced by Ctesias's intimidating one-horned creature, they translated it as *monokeros*, or "single-horned creature," which in the Latin translation of the Septuagint, written mostly by Saint Jerome in the late fourth century A.D., became its Latin equivalent, *unicornis*, or unicorn. Thus the unicorn earned a permanent place in the Bible, which later served as irrefutable proof of its existence, and an important role in most subsequent Christian writing, where the unicorn was firmly identified with Christ. As Saint Basil the Great (ca. 329–375) wrote: "Christ is the power of God, therefore he is called the unicorn because the one horn symbolizes one common power with the Father." And Saint Ambrose (ca. 339–397)

asked: "Who is this unicorn but the only begotten son of God?"

The unicorn acquired far greater importance in European thought after the appearance of a book called the *Physiologus* between the second and fourth centuries A.D. This manuscript collection of stories and legends, written by an author who may have lived in Alexandria, Egypt, as early as A.D. 200, describes real and imaginary animals, including birds, reptiles, and fish, along with the moral lessons they could supposedly teach Christians. According to this work, the fierce and powerful unicorn, which no man or beast could capture, could in fact be tamed by a virgin. Unicorn hunters need only place a young maiden in a part of the forest that a unicorn was known to frequent. Attracted by her scent and her purity, the creature would kneel, place his forelegs and head on her lap, and fall asleep.

Once the maiden's power became known, secular poets and early Christian writers developed a number of allegories in which the unicorn played a major role. The earliest allegories were Christian in form and content, as the image of a fierce, powerful creature being tamed by a virgin inevitably conjured up ideas relating to the Incarnation. A Latin translation of the *Physiologus* was in circulation before the end of the fourth century, by which time its author's name was lost, but the text became

widely known and served as the basis for Latin bestiaries, which became very popular during the Middle Ages. The monks who produced these books describing animals and the religious homilies derived from their habits often quoted the *Physiologus* verbatim, incorporating information from Pliny as well as the Bible. Later versions of the *Physiologus* and these bestiaries continued to associate the story of the unicorn tamed by the maiden with the idea of the Incarnation, and the metaphor persisted into the late Middle Ages. A ninth-century bestiary says in part, "As soon as the unicorn sees [the virgin maiden] he springs into her lap and embraces her. Thus he is taken captive and exhibited in the palace

of the king. . . . In this way Our Lord Jesus Christ, the spiritual unicorn, descended into the womb of the Virgin and through her took on human flesh. . . . And Zacharias says 'He hath raised up an horn of salvation for us in the house of his servant David'" [Luke 1:69]. One bestiary author offered this explanation: "[The unicorn] is very swift because neither principalities, nor powers, nor thrones, nor dominions could keep up with him, nor could Hell contain him, nor could the most subtle devil prevail to catch or contain him;

Figure 8. The Mystic Hunt of the Unicorn. *Tapestry altar frontal, Swiss, about 1480. Zurich, Swiss National Museum*

but, by the sole will of the Father, he came down into the virgin womb for our salvation."

When the modern mind attempts to understand medieval Christian metaphors like these, and indeed when we struggle to isolate one meaning from several that have been combined in a single symbol to express multiple images or thoughts simultaneously (which occurs many times in the three parts of *The Hunt of the Unicorn*), we are obliged to abandon our natural inclination to search for simple logic and even, occasionally, to suspend disbelief.

The capture of the unicorn by the Virgin Mary eventually became standard iconography in Christian art and is now referred to as the Mystic Hunt of the Unicorn. The essential elements are a figure of Gabriel the hunter, blowing his horn and pursuing Christ the unicorn into the Virgin's preserve, the *hortus conclusus* (enclosed garden), where Mary receives the unicorn. In some representations of the Mystic Hunt a nimbed Christ child either rides the unicorn or accompanies a dove of the Holy Spirit as it descends toward the Virgin's head. The subject was extremely popular in the fifteenth century, and some representations are very elaborate (Figure 8). Others, like the one I believe is depicted in the tapestry from which the two Cloisters fragments came (see Figure 27), are quite simple.

When it was still whole, that tapestry may have been designed to hang alone as a visual preface to the story told in *The Hunt of the Unicorn as an Allegory of the Passion* (see Figures 34, 39, 44, 50), a set of four tapestries that depicts another Christian allegory—an even more complex one, in which Christ the unicorn, like the quarry in a contemporary stag hunt, is pursued to the death by hunters and hounds, who symbolize his enemies and tormentors. It is, clearly, a later elaboration of the iconography of the Mystic Hunt of the Unicorn allegory, which is a natural and indeed necessary prelude to it. In his thirteenth-century bestiary Guillaume le Clerc tells how Jesus Christ, the spiritual unicorn, first became incarnate of the Virgin Mary and then suffered persecution and death at the hands of those who did not believe in him. Konrad von Megenberg wrote in his fourteenth-century *Buch der Natur* that Christ, like the unicorn, "was captured by the wicked hunters . . . and by them shamefully put to death."

The four hangings in the Passion group offer us the most elaborate pictorial treatment of this subject known to have been created in the art of tapestry and certainly the only one to have survived into our time. In allegorical terms, these tapestries illustrate Jesus' ministry, betrayal, and passion.

The Start of the Hunt (Figure 16) and *The Unicorn in Captivity* (Figure 23), the only two tapestries in this group of seven that have backgrounds completely strewn with flowering plants (millefleurs), originally belonged to a distinct set of tapestries that illustrated a different kind of unicorn hunt, in this case a secular allegory, a love story. Here, the unicorn represents the Lover; the maiden is his Beloved; and the hunter is Love. This subject was treated not only in tapestries but also in illustrated manuscripts, prints, paintings, and relief carvings.

Figure 9. Miniature painting in a tenth-century manuscript of the
Physiologus. Lower register at left: Jesus addressing two disciples:
"learn of me, for I am meek and lowly in heart" (Matthew 11:29);
at right, a maiden tames a unicorn. Upper register: the maiden leads
the tamed unicorn by the chin to the king's palace. Brussels,
Bibliothèque Royale Albert Ier, Ms. 10066–67, fol. 147

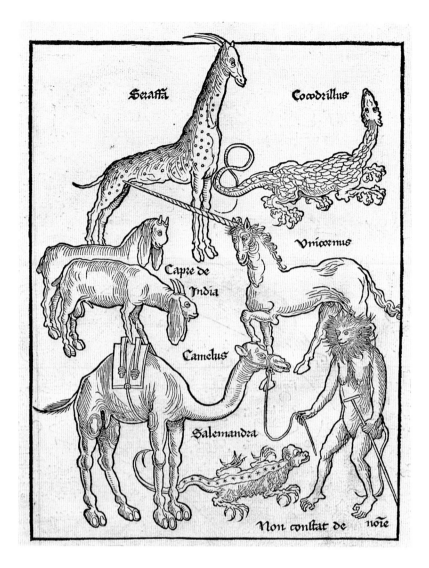

Many contexts seems to be heaven. In a closely related iconography, which does not involve a hunt, the unicorn is presented as a symbol of chastity, an association that probably developed from stories of the unicorn's being attracted to a virgin, both the secular young maiden and the Virgin Mary. Paired unicorns are traditionally shown as the animals drawing the chariot of Chastity in representations of Petrarch's Triumphs.

Given the enormous value placed on the unicorn's horn throughout the Middle Ages, one would naturally expect to find that the kind of unicorn hunt most often represented would be one in which the climax showed hunters taking the creature's horn. Surprisingly enough, that is not the case, even though in some pictures of the capture by a maiden the hunters seem disposed to kill the unicorn (Figure 11). I know of two late-medieval stories, but no visual works of art, that deal with this subject, and this suggests that people who believed in unicorns in the late Middle Ages, and apparently most of them did, were not prepared to reduce it to the status of just another game animal.

As late as 1486 Bernhard von Breydenbach, a dignitary of the cathedral of Mainz, assured the readers of his *Itinerary* that, while on a pilgrimage to the Holy Land in 1483, he and a group of followers saw a unicorn among other strange animals there. The painter he took with him produced a woodcut that illustrates these beasts (Figure 10)—a giraffe, a crocodile,

Other unicorn hunts, which seem to be both secular and religious, have been represented in the visual arts. In one example, the unicorn, after having been tamed by the maiden, was taken to be exhibited "in the palace of the king" (Figure 9), which in

Above: Figure 10. Erhard Reuwich, These Animals are Truly Shown Just as We Saw Them in the Holy Land. *Woodcut illustration for Bernhard von Breydenbach's* Peregrinationes in Montem Syon, *an account of von Breydenbach's pilgrimage in 1483. German (Mainz), 1486. The Metropolitan Museum of Art, Rogers Fund, 1931 (31.54.13)*

Opposite: Figure 11. The Maiden Taming a Unicorn for Two Hunters, *Miniature painting in a manuscript bestiary, about 1170. New York, Pierpont Morgan Library, Ms. 81, fol. 12v*

two Indian goats, a camel, a salamander, a rather anthropomorphic ape, and a unicorn, which does not look out of place in this company. One of the travelers wrote another account of the same trip and reported that they had seen an animal grazing at a distance and thought it was a camel, but their guide, calling attention to the creature's single horn, told them it was a unicorn.

The unicorn's existence and its significance as a Christian symbol began to come under theological and scientific scrutiny in the mid-sixteenth century. In 1563 the Council of Trent looked with disfavor on such allusions to Christ and concluded that they should not be represented in works of art. Three years later, Andrea Marini, an Italian scholar, wrote that he believed that

no one had ever seen a unicorn and that the "horn" was in fact the tusk of a sea animal. Gerhardus Mercator identified the "horn" as the tusk of the narwhal in his atlas of 1621.

In the early nineteenth century, a French zoologist finally exploded the myth of the unicorn by noting that the skull of cloven-hoofed creatures was divided in the center and therefore that no horn could grow there. Early in the twentieth century, an American doctor, having discovered that the horn buds of a bull could be transplanted to the center of the skull, produced a single-horned bull calf. It was probably this procedure that was used in the 1980s on a domestic goat to produce a "unicorn" that appeared as a popular circus attraction, a sad conclusion to the unicorn's remarkable story.

The Three Hunts of the Unicorn

Although the hunts depicted in these tapestries involve a unicorn as the quarry, the huntsmen are engaged in procedures that were typically followed in medieval stag hunts. Since the men depended primarily on dogs and only incidentally on weapons to capture the stag, this sport was called hunting "by force of hounds." The method was described in a number of treatises on game hunting written in the fourteenth century. The one best known today is the *Livre de Chasse* (*Hunting Book*) written by Gaston III, comte de Foix, toward the end of the fourteenth century (Figure 12). The author, because he was extraordinarily handsome, was popularly referred to as "Gaston Phébus," an allusion to Phoebus (Apollo), the beautiful god of the sun. Gaston's book was written for members of the royalty and nobility, the classes who had the wealth and the leisure to hunt game animals for sport.

In the third of four books of Gaston Phébus's manuscript, he describes a hunt by force of hounds down to the smallest detail.

Figure 12. Miniature painting of an episode in a late-medieval stag hunt from a manuscript of the Livre de Chasse *by Gaston III, comte de Foix (Gaston Phébus). French, early fifteenth century. Paris, Bibliothèque Nationale de France, Ms. fr. 616, fol. 68*

Opposite: Figure 13. Detail of The Unicorn Is Killed (*Figure 50*)

Figure 14. The Stag at Bay. *Tapestry, Southern Netherlands, 1495–1515. The Metropolitan Museum of Art, Bequest of Helen Hay Whitney, 1944 (45.128.21)*

This description served as a guide not only for practicing hunters of the day but also for writers and designers facing the problem of representing a typical medieval hunt, whether for a stag, a wild boar, or, as in this case, a unicorn.

Three sets of tapestries in the Museum's collection show stag hunts by force of hounds. They were all woven about the same time as *The Hunt of the Unicorn*, but only one of these sets deals with a real stag hunt. It shows several stages in the hunt as described by Gaston Phébus, some of them corresponding to incidents in the hunt of the unicorn. Compare, for example, the moment when the hounds have cornered the stag and hold it at bay until the lord of the hunt can ride in and deliver the death blow (Figure 14) with the similar moment in the unicorn hunt (Figure 15).

The other two stag hunts in the Museum do not depict a real hunt but the allegory of *Le Cerf Fragile* (The Frail Stag), a hunt in which the stag is the symbol of Everyman, who proceeds through life from birth to death and faces trials at every step of the way. He is assailed in his progress by the characters Old Age, Ignorance, Illness, and Vanity and by the hounds Rashness, Desire, Anxiety, Fear, Grief, and many others. In both sets of tapestries there are pieces representing episodes that correspond to moments in *The Hunt of the Unicorn*. For example, in both hunts the quarry, having thrown itself into a body of water to cool off and to break the trail of its scent, leaps out of the water on the opposite shore in the hope of eluding its pursuers (Figures 39, 40).

Figure 15. Detail of The Unicorn at Bay *(Figure 44)*

THE HUNT OF THE UNICORN AS LOVER

The first of the two pieces in the Museum's set of tapestries, *The Start of the Hunt* (Figure 16), shows a flowery meadow in which five hunters and their hounds walk toward a wood at the right as they start out on the hunt. The three men at the left, dressed in rich velvets and brocaded silks and wearing plumed hats, are three nobles or gentlemen who, as guests of the host for the day's hunting, are out to enjoy the sport. All three men wear swords; two of them also carry spears and the third has a hunting horn. The more simply dressed

men at the right are the professional hunters, the "lymerers" who train and care for the hounds and structure the stages of the hunt according to the dogs' behavior and progress. Both lymerers have hunting horns; the one at the right also has a spear. Although the guest at the far left has his own greyhound, it is the lymerer's paired greyhounds and scent hounds that will do most of the work on this hunt.

The letters AE (the E reversed), knotted together with a plied and tasseled cord, appear in the four corners of the compo-

Above: *Figure 16.* The Start of the Hunt, *from* The Hunt of the Unicorn as Lover. *Southern Netherlands, 1495–1505. Wool warp; wool, silk, silver, and gilt wefts. Height 12 feet, 1 inch; width 10 feet, 4 inches (3.68 x 3.15 meters). Gift of John D. Rockefeller Jr., 1937 (37.80.1)*

Opposite: *Figure 17.* The Start of the Hunt, *detail showing three guest hunters*

sition and also tied to the branches of a cherry tree in the middle distance left of center (Figure 18). The letters AE (the E not reversed) without the cord are embroidered on the collar of one of the lymerer's greyhounds, and the letter A alone, shown twice, alternating with a shield of arms, appears on the collar of the other hound of this pair (Figure 19). The two letters tied together constitute the cipher, or monogram, of the person or persons for whom all seven of the *Hunt of the Unicorn* tapestries were woven. The letters in some ciphers of this kind represent the initials of the given and family names of one person; in other

Above: Figure 18. The Start of the Hunt, detail showing the cipher AE tied to a wild cherry tree

Opposite: Figure 19. The Start of the Hunt, detail showing two of the greyhounds. The collar worn by the one in the foreground is marked AE; the other is marked with the letter A alternating with an unidentified shield of arms

cases the letters are the initials of the given names of a husband and wife. Such a cipher, showing N and G tied with a knotted and tasseled cord, appears in the corners of another millefleurs tapestry in the Museum, one that we know was woven for Nicolas Bouesseau and his wife, Guillemette (Figure 20).

In *The Start of the Hunt* the sport has already begun. The scout perched high in a distant tree at the right raises his right hand to signal that he has found the quarry in its lair. Because the next scene in a hunt by force of hounds would normally show the hunters finding the quarry in its den, it is not surprising that this tapestry has always been thought to precede the one showing the hunters coming upon the unicorn dipping its horn in the stream, and therefore that this scene is part of *The Hunt of the Unicorn as an Allegory of the Passion*. That story, however, is the subject of a separate set of tapestries, of which only four pieces have survived (see Figures 34, 39, 44, 50). There is a marked stylistic difference between those four pieces and the two that belong to *The Hunt of the Unicorn as the Lover*. Specialists who believe that all six hangings belong to one and the same set have made various attempts to explain away this difference. It has been suggested that the two pieces from the Unicorn-as-Lover set were added to the other four at a later date, or that they were woven at the same time but designed by a different artist or perhaps woven in a different shop by less skillful workers. Certainly the two love-story pieces were designed by a different hand. The plants and trees are drawn

slightly differently, and the facial types, heavy and inexpressive, have nothing to do with the highly individualized and animated faces in the other four hangings. But these two tapestries are just as finely woven as the others; they simply belong to a different set of hangings.

We do not know how many episodes were originally represented in the Unicorn-as-Lover set nor how many pieces it com-

Above: Figure 20. Cipher with the letters N *and* G *knotted together with a plied and tasseled cord, for Nicolas Bouesseau and his wife, Guillemette. Detail of tapestry* Five Youths Playing Blindman's Buff. *Southern Netherlands, 1500–1525. The Metropolitan Museum of Art, Bequest of Adele L. Lehman, in memory of Arthur Lehman, 1965 (65.181.17)*

Opposite: Figure 21. The Start of the Hunt, *detail showing the scout posted in the trees signaling to the hunters*

prised. There would have been one or more scenes showing the hunters trying to subdue the unicorn with their hounds or overcoming the beast by having a maiden tame it. Even then, with the unicorn subdued and rendered harmless, the hunters might still attack it. Such a scene is depicted on the end of a fourteenth-century French carved ivory jewel box (Figure 22). However, the wounds that the hunter inflicts, which are visible in *The Unicorn in Captivity* (Figure 23), do the creature no harm. As strange as this seems to us, it undoubtedly made perfect sense at the time the tapestries were woven. Everyone knew that the hunter in this tale of the unicorn represented the personification of Love and that the wounds he inflicted, like the darts of Cupid, did no physical harm. Therefore, the conquered unicorn can appear entirely alive, despite its wounds, in the last

Figure 22. End panel of a carved ivory jewel box, Love, the Hunter, Spears the Unicorn, the Lover, *next to a scene showing an episode in the story of Tristan and Isolde. French, fourteenth century. Baltimore, The Walters Art Gallery*

Opposite: Figure 23. The Unicorn in Captivity, *from* The Hunt of the Unicorn as Lover. *Southern Netherlands, 1495–1505. Wool warp; wool, silk, silver, and gilt wefts. Height 12 feet, 1 inch; width 8 feet, 3 inches (3.68 x 2.52 meters). Gift of John D. Rockefeller Jr., 1937 (37.80.6)*

tapestry of the set. He, the Lover, has been subdued by his Beloved, the maiden, with the help of the hunter, Love. The Beloved then chains the Lover to a tree, an action symbolizing his commitment to her in marriage. That moment, which anticipates the scene in *The Unicorn in Captivity*, appears in a Florentine engraving made a generation or so earlier than the tapestry (Figure 24). There we see the maiden fondling the enraptured unicorn's neck with one hand while she brings the chained collar around with the other to tie about the creature's neck. *The Unicorn in Captivity* shows the final moment in the allegory: the unicorn-Lover now lives happily in a garden of delight, chained to a pomegranate tree, which symbolizes marriage and fertility.

Figure 24. Engraving showing the unicorn's beloved, Marietta, about to place a chained collar around its neck. Italian (Florence), about 1465–80. London, The British Museum

Because these two tapestries, unlike the other five in *The Hunt of the Unicorn*, have millefleurs backgrounds, it is necessary to consider the flora represented in them in slightly different terms. They show a greater variety of plants than the other five pieces do, although those plants are not so accurately rendered. The tree in the center of *The Unicorn in Captivity* bears fruits that are unmistakably pomegranates, but the foliage does not resemble that of the pomegranate tree (Figure 25). On the other hand, the trees in *The Start of the Hunt* are correctly rendered cherry, English elm, oak, linden, walnut, and plum trees. The flowering plants in both pieces include the daffodil, carnation, wallflower, sweet violet, campion, English daisy, white thistle, stock, gillyflower, marigold, bluebell, wild strawberry, periwinkle, Madonna lily, iris, rose, and columbine (see Appendix 1). These were all well-known, popular plants of the period, many of which were loved for their scent. Most of the flowers, especially the rose, violet, carnation, and Madonna lily, were regarded as symbols of the Virgin. Others, like periwinkle and white thistle, were believed to ward off evil; and wild strawberries were thought of as the food of the blessed. So, while the choice and placement of these plants may not have had specific symbolic meaning in these two tapestries—nor indeed in the other five as well—medieval viewers of the flora in *The Hunt of the Unicorn* enjoyed the splendor of the sight, the illusion of the scent, and the pleasure of knowing that, in their culture, these plants carried comforting or inspiring messages.

Figure 25. The Unicorn in Captivity, *detail showing the top of the pomegranate tree and the cipher AE*

Overleaf: Figure 26. The Unicorn in Captivity, *detail showing some of the flowering plants outside the enclosure. In the back row left to right: carnation, iris, and an unidentified plant. In the foreground: top of a wallflower, white thistle, and Madonna lily*

The Mystic Hunt of the Unicorn

The two fragmentary tapestries (Figure 27) that were acquired for The Cloisters in 1938 came from a hanging that, until recently, was thought to show another incident in the story of *The Hunt of the Unicorn*, an episode where the hunters, finding that they cannot capture the unicorn by force of hounds, place a virgin in the forest to tame the creature for them. However, there are a number of arguments against this interpretation. First, there are significant differences in style between this composition and those in the four main tapestries of the unicorn hunt. The facial type of the young woman standing at the left, the drawing of the bit of the letter A in the cipher AE that hangs mostly out of view on the apple tree at the far right, the static quality of this composition—these all differ from the style of corresponding elements in the four main hunting tapestries. Also, the piece of guard band running along the outside edge of the left-hand fragment has an inner stripe of red, whereas the corresponding stripe along the lower left side of the tapestry showing the unicorn leaping up out of the river (see Figure 39) is white. This alone is enough to indicate that the two fragments, although themselves part of the same hanging, came from a different set of tapestries than the four passion pieces.

Even more significant than these differences is a telling iconographical non sequitur. In the tapestry showing the unicorn defending itself (see Figure 44), the nine hunters and twelve hounds are holding the unicorn at bay. They have it completely surrounded, and it has no chance of escaping. Furthermore, we are told in a thirteenth-century encyclopedia by Thomas de Cantimpré that the Unicorn-as-Christ allows his pursuers to capture him. Why then would these hunters cancel the hunt at this point and begin all over again by having a maiden subdue the unicorn they have already subdued? There would be no point in hunting the unicorn by force of hounds in the first place if the creature could be captured so simply with the help of a maiden. Indeed, some medieval bestiaries, such as Richard de Fournival's *Bestiaire d'Amour*, observed that the hunters would never attack a unicorn awake, because they knew they couldn't capture it. They would approach the unicorn only after a maiden had put it to sleep.

The unicorn represented in these two tapestry fragments is obviously entranced by the woman whose right hand caresses its neck. It can be safely concluded, therefore, that the tapestry from which the fragments came shows a moment in some story where a unicorn is being hunted with the aid of a maiden. In the mythology of the unicorn, maidens are used to entrap the creature for a number of different reasons. As we have

Figure 27. Two fragments from a lost tapestry of The Mystic Hunt of the Unicorn. *Southern Netherlands, 1495–1505. Wool warp; wool, silk, silver, and gilt wefts. At the left, height 5 feet, 6½ inches; width 2 feet, 1½ inches (1.69 x .65 meters). At the right, height 6 feet, 6½ inches; width 2 feet, 1½ inches (1.99 x .65 meters). Gift of John D. Rockefeller Jr., 1937 (38.51.1,2)*

already seen, the girl may represent the Beloved, the unicorn her Lover, and the hunter or hunters Love. A different iconography deals with the maiden who helps to capture the unicorn so that it can be taken alive to be exhibited "in the palace of the king," as many medieval bestiaries tell the tale (Figures 9, 28). Another hunt using the lure of a maiden is a rare one I know only from a literary source, the *Physica*, written in the twelfth century by the German abbess Hildegard of Bingen. In that story, several maidens distract the unicorn, which is then easily slain by the hunters who kill it and remove the horn as a prize.

However, the maiden-capture pictured in the Museum's two tapestry fragments is not one of those. The image, incomplete though it is, contains particular details suggesting that the hanging from which the

fragments came was a specific depiction of *The Mystic Hunt of the Unicorn*, where Gabriel the hunter causes Christ the unicorn to enter the *hortus conclusus*, succumb to Mary, and so become incarnate. The prominence of the white and red roses, the choice of an apple tree to rise in the center of the composition, the fact that the acting space is enclosed by a fence (the *hortus conclusus*), and the treacherous aspect of the young woman signaling to the hunter (who

Above: Figure 28. Engraving showing the maiden and hunters capturing the tamed unicorn alive by tying it to two trees. One of six unicorn prints by Jean Duvet. French, 1540–60. London, The British Museum

Opposite: Figure 29. Right-hand fragment of The Mystic Hunt of the Unicorn, *detail showing the head of the treacherous young woman (Eve?)*

may represent Gabriel)—all of these details encourage us to believe that this is a representation of *The Mystic Hunt of the Unicorn*.

The composition in the original tapestry was large enough to show whatever additional figures, plants, and objects might have been necessary to illustrate this subject more clearly. Using the dimensions of the seven tapestries given in the 1680 inventory of comte François VI de La Rochefoucauld, I calculate that the two fragments came from a hanging that was approximately 10 feet, 6 inches (3.20 meters) wide and, like the other six hangings, about 15 feet, 9 inches (4.90 meters) tall. The two fragments together, as mounted at the Museum, measure 4 feet, 6 inches (1.32 meters) across, or somewhat less than half the width of the whole tapestry. The height of the two fragments represents a bit

Figure 30. Detail of tapestry altar frontal in Figure 8 showing Gabriel

more than half the height of the original tapestry. It is clear then that these two fragments show slightly less than the upper left quarter of the original composition. Obviously, a number of important details in the composition have been lost. Nevertheless, what has been preserved suggests that the whole tapestry showed a simplified version of a typical fifteenth-century *Mystic Hunt of the Unicorn*.

The most elaborate representation of this subject that I know appears in a Swiss tapestry altar frontal dating from about 1480 (Figures 8, 30, 32). The archangel Gabriel, wearing a chaplet of roses on his head and dressed as a hunter with a horn, a spear, and a double pair of hounds, sweeps in from the left and addresses the Virgin, who is seated in her enclosed garden at the far right, with the classic words of the Annunciation: *Ave maria gratia plena dominus tecum*. His hounds are labeled *veritas*, *justitia*, *pax*, and *misericordia* (Truth, Justice, Peace, and Mercy), representing the Four Daughters of God, who, in early-medieval mystery plays, argue either for or against Man, as the Trinity considers whether to punish the children of Adam for their sins or to return them to Paradise. Finally, Christ offers to become incarnate and by so doing to redeem humanity.

The hunter Gabriel and his hounds have found the unicorn and chased it into the enclosed garden to be tamed (that is, made incarnate) by the Virgin Mary (Figure 33). She holds the spotted creature's horn, and from the clouds above a tiny haloed Christ child and a dove of the Holy Spirit descend

toward her head. The enclosed garden and the open space at the left end of the composition are crammed with roses, lilies, and other flowers identified with the Virgin Mary, as well as with symbols referring to her attributes, including, among many others, the locked gate, the flowering rod of Aaron, the tower of David, Gideon's fleece, the well of living water, and the mirror without stain. The iconography is unusual in that it shows tiny figures of Adam and Eve next to the unicorn. Adam says, as he thrusts a spear into the unicorn's chest, "He is wounded because of our sins," while Eve, standing below the wound and collecting the unicorn's blood in a chalice, answers, "And by his blood we are saved." Finally, there is a symbolic reference to the Resurrection. A lion at the left end of the composition roars at his cubs to bring them to life. A pelican feeding her young with blood from her breast, a symbol of Charity, appears inside the *hortus conclusus*, just left of center.

Figure 31. Left-hand fragment of The Mystic Hunt of the Unicorn, *detail showing the hunter outside the enclosure sounding his horn (the archangel Gabriel?)*

The two fragments of tapestry in The Cloisters show some of these details. The lost parts of the original composition may have shown more. The wooden fence encloses the *hortus conclusus* and supports a profusion of white and red roses, which are symbols of the Virgin—white for her purity, red for her charity. The apple tree was displayed prominently in the center of the composition. This is surely the Tree of the Knowledge of Good and Evil, which grew in the Garden of Eden. In the foreground, the unicorn's body appears in an attitude that suggests it is crouching before the woman who caresses its neck (Figure 33), and the creature seems to smile as it gazes into her face. The hunter who stands outside the enclosure at the left, sounding his horn, may represent Gabriel (Figure 31). Two of his four hounds (representing the Four Daughters of God?) are still with him; the other two have entered the garden and attacked the unicorn. The young woman standing near the unicorn, who steals a glance at the hunter and signals to him with her left hand, is probably Eve (Figure 29). Adam may have been represented opposite her in the right end of the enclosed garden.

Since the Museum's fragmented tapestry in its original form illustrated a subject whose content can be expressed in a single image describing a single moment, it seems likely that it was never part of a set of hangings. It was probably produced either as a devotional piece to be contemplated by itself, like the many paintings and tapestry altar frontals that show the same subject, or, more likely, as a single hanging to introduce

the pieces in the cycle of *The Hunt of the Unicorn as an Allegory of the Passion*. This tapestry would provide the first episode—the Incarnation of Christ—in the story of Christ's ministry and Passion. If this is true, the monumental stability of the composition in the lost tapestry—contrasted to the dynamic compositions that show the stages of the hunt—seems most appropriate.

Although, as noted above, there are a number of stylistic discrepancies that set these two fragments apart from the four extant *Hunt of the Unicorn as an Allegory of the Passion* hangings, the tapestry from which the fragments came nevertheless shows the AE cipher and must therefore have been woven for the same patron or patrons.

Above: Figure 32. The Mystic Hunt of the Unicorn, *detail of tapestry altar frontal in Figure 8 showing virgin and unicorn*

Opposite: Figure 33. The Mystic Hunt of the Unicorn, *detail of Figure 27 showing the Virgin's hand on the unicorn's neck*

Figure 34. The Unicorn Is Found, *from* The Hunt of the
Unicorn as an Allegory of the Passion. *Southern Netherlands,
1495–1505. Wool warp; wool, silk, silver, and gilt wefts. Height
12 feet, 1 inch; width 12 feet, 5 inches (3.68 x 3.79 meters). Gift of
John D. Rockefeller Jr., 1937 (37.80.2)*

Opposite: Figure 35. The Unicorn Is Found, *detail showing the
unicorn dipping its horn into the stream in front of the fountain's
basin*

The Hunt of the Unicorn as an Allegory of the Passion

There may have been more than four hangings in the set of tapestries from which these pieces came (Figures 34, 39, 44, 50). One would expect that the cycle might begin with a piece showing the hunters setting out on the unicorn hunt and end with the Resurrection, but if tapestries with those subjects were ever woven, they have been lost. However, as noted below, there are both iconographic and formal details in these four pieces that suggest the set may be complete as it is.

The Unicorn Is Found

Like the compositions in *The Hunt of the Unicorn as Lover* and the *Mystic Hunt,* these hangings show figures arranged around a dominant central motif. In this piece (Figure 34), the motif is a marble fountain whose central pillar is decorated with carved trefoils, gilt lion-head spouts, and a gilt finial in the shape of a pomegranate. The water that collects in the basin spills out through the mouth of a gilt lion mask below and feeds a stream running

Figure 36. The Unicorn Is Found, *detail showing the pillar spout in the fountain, the cipher AE, the pair of pheasants, and a group of hunters in conversation*

Opposite: Figure 37. The Unicorn Is Found, *detail showing the hunters in the background*

across the foreground. A pair of pheasants and a pair of goldfinches perch on the rim of the basin. The unicorn, a creature smaller than a full-grown horse, kneels in front of the fountain and bends forward to dip the end of its horn into the stream. Five wild creatures rest on the near shore of the stream. They are, left to right, a pair of lions, a panther, a genet, and a hyena. A stag with a fine pair of antlers leaps up from behind a small orange tree in the right foreground. A castle set beyond a slope of turf in the far distance appears through a break in the trees in the upper left corner of the composition.

The cipher AE hangs on the pillar at the center of the fountain (Figure 36). Four more ciphers are displayed against the foliage in the four corners of the composition. The letters, worked in silver yarns, resemble the ones in the *Mystic Hunt* (Figure 27), but these letters are slimmer and somewhat taller. They differ also from the letters in *The Start of the Hunt* and *The Unicorn in Captivity*. In those tapestries, the letters are shaped differently, and they are woven with red rather than silver yarns.

The hunters are engaged in an animated discussion. Their gestures indicate that they realize they are witnessing something more significant than simply the sight of their quarry in its lair. They seem to be pulling back in order to watch, and not interrupt, the sacred action taking place before them. Early bestiaries indicate that the unicorn dips its horn into water that wild creatures need for drinking in order to purify it of the poisons that serpents have spewed into it. The allegory is clear: Christ takes on the

sins of Man, and so purifies him, in order to bring about his redemption. The serpent is the devil; the poison he introduces into the world (the water) is sin.

There may be other symbolic elements here. The most significant one, almost surely introduced deliberately, is the red cabbage-rose bush that grows directly behind the unicorn. Red roses are symbols of martyrdom and of Christ, as well as of the Virgin Mary. In this instance, the red-rose bush probably was placed next to the unicorn to emphasize its relation to Christ and to his martyrdom. Some of the flowering plants that grow in the foreground—including the English daisy and pot marigold (see page 112)—are symbolic of the Virgin, and the marigold was also credited with having power against poisons.

It has always been assumed that the hunter in the left foreground who points at the unicorn and speaks to the man at his left is simply calling attention to the quarry and its curious activity. However, he may be more significant than that. A cycle of mural paintings that Antoine, duc de Lorraine, commissioned in 1524 for his palace at Nancy showed twenty-two scenes comparing the life of a stag to the life of Christ, from the birth of a fawn to the death of a stag at the hands of hunters, and from the Nativity to the Crucifixion. The metaphor of the stag hunt enters the iconography at the point where Judas betrays Christ. It is legitimate to ask, then,

Opposite: Figure 38. The Unicorn Is Found, *detail showing the lymerer (Judas?) pointing to the unicorn*

whether this pointing hunter in the unicorn tapestry is meant to represent Judas in allegorical terms. If that is so, it may be assumed that this hanging, and not some lost one depicting the hunters setting out, serves as the beginning of *The Hunt of the Unicorn as an Allegory of the Passion*.

The Unicorn Leaps out of the Stream

The episode shown in the second hanging of this set (Figure 39) takes place a while after the hunters find the unicorn. These are not the same men who watched the creature from behind the screen of trees in the last tapestry—the cast of characters changes from piece to piece in these four hangings. Nevertheless, we are meant to understand that this is the same hunting party. The men have pursued the unicorn through the forest, following the hounds, until the quarry jumps into a river to try to elude the hunters and to cool off. But some of the hounds have taken to the water as well, and others are being released ("slipped") from the shore. A bleeding wound on the unicorn's rump shows that a hound has managed to attack it before the plunge.

This is one of the customary stages in a hunt by force of hounds. Gaston Phébus mentions it in his book on the subject, and it is often depicted in representations of medieval stag hunts. It appears, for exam-

Figure 39. The Unicorn Leaps out of the Stream, *from* The Hunt of the Unicorn as an Allegory of the Passion. *Southern Netherlands, 1495–1505. Wool warp; wool, silk, silver, and gilt wefts. Height 12 feet, 1 inch; width 14 feet (3.68 x 4.27 meters). Gift of John D. Rockefeller Jr., 1937 (37.80.3)*

ple, in both of the Museum's sets of tapestries dealing with the subject of the Hunt of the Frail Stag (Figure 40). In those hangings, the body of water looks more like a lake than a river. However, Gaston writes that the stag seeks refuge in a river, and the designer of this tapestry gives the creature a wide tributary of the fountain-fed stream to jump into. But the ruse does not work. Three of the scent hounds have followed the unicorn into the water, and two greyhounds and four hunters have anticipated the escape attempt and positioned themselves on the far embankment to engage the unicorn as it emerges from the river.

One of the AE ciphers is tied to the trunk of an oak tree that grows on the near shore of the stream in the center of the composition. Another cipher is shown against foliage in each of the four corners of the composition, against oak leaves at the right and holly leaves at the left. A different cipher, consisting of the letters F and R knotted together with a plied and tasseled cord, has been sewn to the modern material representing the sky directly above the central oak tree. This cipher, which has been interpreted as one belonging to François I de La Rochefoucauld, who lived in the latter part of the fifteenth century, differs in color, style, and weaving from the AE emblem and does not belong to *The Hunt of the Unicorn* tapestries.

The break in the trees, which gives a view into the far distance, like the opening in the preceding hanging, occurs here in the upper right corner of the composition, rather than the left. The castle that appears there shares a number of architectural fea-

tures with the first castle and may be intended to represent the same structure. It has been suggested that the oak and holly trees in *The Hunt of the Unicorn* have special symbolic significance. Certainly in this hanging those two varieties of tree far outnumber the others, which include the medlar, hazel, pomegranate, wild plum, and wild cherry (see page 113).

Above: Figure 40. Old Age Drives the Stag out of a Lake. Tapestry fragment, Southern Netherlands, 1495–1510. The Metropolitan Museum of Art, Bequest of Adele L. Lehman, in memory of Arthur Lehman, 1965 (65.181.20)

Opposite: Figure 41. The Unicorn Leaps out of the Stream, detail showing the hunters and hounds poised to attack the unicorn as it leaps ashore

Figure 42. The Unicorn Leaps out of the Stream, *details showing the AE and FR ciphers*

Opposite: Figure 43. The Unicorn Leaps out of the Stream, *detail showing the castle beyond the hill in the background*

Figure 44. The Unicorn at Bay, *from* The Hunt of the Unicorn as an Allegory of the Passion. *Southern Netherlands, 1495–1505. Wool warp; wool, silk, silver, and gilt wefts. Height 12 feet, 1 inch; width 13 feet, 2 inches (3.68 x 4.01 meters). Gift of John D. Rockefeller Jr., 1937 (37.80.4)*

The Unicorn at Bay

In the third tapestry (Figure 44) the attack on the unicorn accelerates. Three hunters, one behind the creature and two in front, are holding it at bay, their spears poised to pierce its body. The unicorn, trying desperately to escape its tormentors, kicks its hind legs out at the back and gores one of the greyhounds in the foreground with its sharp horn. The other hounds, now whipped into a frenzy, jump up all around the cornered beast. This corresponds to the moment in a conventional stag hunt when the quarry is trapped and held at bay until the kill can be made. This moment is also illustrated in one of the hangings from the Museum's set of secular stag-hunting tapestries (Figure 14). In that example, it is the hounds that attack the quarry while the hunters hang back to allow the mounted hunter at the right, the master of the hunt, to approach out of the stag's line of sight and deliver the coup de grâce with his sword.

There is a hunter in the left foreground of *The Unicorn at Bay*—the one standing on the far shore of the stream (Figure 46)—who has a scabbard inscribed with the words AVE REGINA C[OELORUM] (Hail, Queen of the Heavens) and is blowing his horn. This is certainly the archangel Gabriel, even though he usually begins his annunciation of the Incarnation to Mary with the words "Ave Maria, gratia plena . . ." Gabriel's presence here, in a scene that is surely not an Annunciation, is indeed significant but also enigmatic. Is Gabriel sounding the "cornure à l'aide" (call for help), or has he returned to the world at this moment to announce the impending

Figure 45. The Unicorn at Bay, detail of Figure 44

Figure 46. The Unicorn at Bay, *detail showing the hunter with the scabbard inscribed* AVE REGINA C[OELORUM] *(Gabriel) and the greyhound with the collar marked* OFANCRE

Opposite: *Figure 47.* The Unicorn at Bay, *detail showing the unicorn goring a hound with its horn*

Figure 48. The Unicorn at Bay, *detail showing the hunter and hounds in the background*

death of Christ, just as he came to announce his birth? I know of no precedent for such an iconography; it would be an extremely rare but not impossible one.

In this third episode of the allegorical unicorn hunt, one of the AE ciphers is tied to the branches of an orange tree that rises in the middle distance at the center of the composition (Figure 48). Another cipher appears in each corner of the field, against a forget-me-not plant at lower left, a peach tree lower right, an apricot upper right, and, in the upper left corner, in front of the distant turf below the castle (Figure

49). Again, this could be the same castle but seen from a different angle. An oak and a holly grow in the upper left part of the composition, but they are not as prominently displayed as they are in the preceding tapestry. This suggests that they may not be so significant in terms of symbolism here as they may have been in the other hanging.

Figure 49. The Unicorn at Bay, *detail showing the castle beyond the hill in the background and the AE cipher*

Figure 50. The Unicorn Is Killed and Brought to the Castle, *from*
The Hunt of the Unicorn as an Allegory of the Passion. *Southern
Netherlands, 1495–1505. Wool warp; wool, silk, silver, and gilt wefts.
Height 12 feet, 1 inch; width 12 feet, 9 inches (3.68 x 3.89 meters). Gift
of John D. Rockefeller Jr., 1937 (37.80.5)*

The Unicorn Is Killed and Brought to the Castle

The last tapestry in this set shows two major episodes in the story (Figure 50). The first, representing the death of the unicorn at the hands of the hunters, is played out on a forested hillside that rises in the middle distance at the left. The creature is trapped between two hunters thrusting spears into its neck and chest from the front and four hounds who bite, growl, and jump up at it from behind. The host of the day's sport slinks in quietly from the rear, keeping out of the unicorn's sight, to deliver the death blow with his sword. This is done precisely according to Gaston Phébus's description of the death of a stag. The hunter in the left middle ground now does his part in the hunt by blowing on his horn the notes that signal the death of the quarry.

The more important episode is played out in the foreground. Three hunters, with their hounds, enter from the left. The man in the middle of this group walks beside the dead unicorn, which has been slung across the back of a horse exactly as a dead stag would be brought back to the castle at the end of a successful stag hunt (Figures 53, 54). This hunter grasps the unicorn's horn with his left hand and, as he addresses the hunter walking next to him, gestures with his right hand toward the richly dressed man and woman standing at the head of a procession coming out of the castle at the right. Another castle, the one beyond the sloping turf, which appears in the backgrounds of the other three tapestries in this set, may be seen in the far distance at the center of this composition.

The cipher AE appears in this tapestry in the upper and lower left corners of the field but not in the lower right corner, where fragments of later tapestry fabric showing floral motifs were used to restore that lost part of the hanging. In the upper right corner of this composition only the A and tasseled cord survive from the cipher that was there originally. Apparently, the reversed E was cut away with the original fabric representing the sky when it was removed in the period before the looted tapestries were returned to the château de Verteuil in the 1850s.

Holly, oak, and elm trees grow behind the scene showing the attack on the unicorn, and a hawthorn rises directly behind the dead creature in the middle ground. It may be significant that these trees appear here; for the hawthorn and the holly are traditionally associated with the Crown of Thorns, and the crown or wreath that ties the dead unicorn's horn to its neck is made of oak branches that have sprouted thorns.

The episode in the foreground has traditionally been interpreted as one simply showing the dead unicorn brought back to the castle. However, the unicorn's crown or wreath of thorned oak and the expressions and gestures of the pointing hunter and of the lord and lady invite a more significant interpretation. In a recent study of *The Hunt of the Unicorn*, the oak and holly have been associated with pagan myths of death and resurrection. Therefore, the presence in this scene of oak and holly trees and of the thorny oak wreath are particularly telling.

Finally, it is difficult to ignore the fact that the lord and lady at this castle wear

Figure 51. The Unicorn Is Killed, *detail showing the hunters killing the unicorn and sounding the death notes*

Figure 52. The Unicorn Is Killed, *detail in which the dead unicorn is brought to the castle on the back of a horse*

ΒL Deceber habet dies. xxxi. Lu
na. xxx.

		f	eligii epi	xvii	A	
xiii		g	bibiane	vi	b	graciani
ii		A			c	
x		b	barbare	xiiii	d	Vigilia.
		c	sabbe	iii	e	Thome apli.
xviii		d	Nicolai epi		f	
vii		e	ambrosii	xi	g	
		f	Coce. ma.	xix	A	Vigilia
xv		g			b	Natitas dni.
iiii		A	culalie	viii	c	Stephai pth.
		b	damasi		d	Iohanis apli.
xii		c		xvi	e	Sctoru inoce.
i		d	lucie	v	f	thome mart.
		e			g	
ix		f		xiii	A	siluestri pape
		g				

Est tibi barbara nicol peeptio virginis e sol.
Festa dehic thoe colo nat stephi o puerisq.
Eloy sait bar ba co lart
Ma rie cri e lu ce art.
Dont en grant i re tho mas meut.
De No. E. ihan In no centfut.

expressions of great sorrow, that the lady is saying her rosary, and that three women stand just behind them. These details suggest that there is a deeper meaning here, that we are in fact witnessing the Deposition in company with the Virgin, John the Evangelist, the three Marys, and the other followers of Christ who were on Calvary at that moment. There is another reading, however. The couple's sorrow and the fact that the huntsman holding the dead unicorn's horn points to the man and woman perhaps accusingly, as though they were responsible for the death (which as lord and lady of the castle they would indeed be if this were a secular stag hunt) may indicate instead that the designer meant us to perceive the lord and lady as Adam and Eve. When they appear as sinners in representations of the Mystic Hunt of the Unicorn (see Figure 8), they acknowledge that they have caused the death of the Unicorn-as-Christ and that through his blood mankind is saved.

The composition at this end of the tapestry turns around on itself and does not invite the eye to go on reading the narrative from left to right. On the other hand, the composition at the left end of the piece is open and does invite the eye into the scene. This suggests that the designer did not intend to add another tapestry, one depicting the Resurrection, to hang to the right of this one. Furthermore, I do not know of any late-medieval representation of a resurrected unicorn. It would be conceptually difficult, if not impossible, to show such a scene when the unicorn in this set of hangings has been so completely identified with a stag. Therefore I conclude, at least tentatively, that there never was a Unicorn Resurrected tapestry in *The Hunt of the Unicorn*.

Above: Figure 53. Detail of woodcut in Figure 54

Opposite: Figure 54. Woodcut showing scenes from a stag hunt in the left and bottom borders; the dead stag carried on a horse appears at the bottom. From a book of hours published by Thielman Kerver, French (Paris), 1504. The Metropolitan Museum of Art, Rogers Fund, 1920 (20.53.3)

Figure 55. The Unicorn Is Killed, *detail showing the castle of the host of the hunt*

Opposite: Figure 56. The Unicorn Is Killed, *detail showing the lord and lady of the castle (John and Mary? Adam and Eve?)*

The Tapestries as Works of Art and How They Were Made

The *Hunt of the Unicorn* hangings, like others of their time, were meant to serve as coverings for the walls of rooms in one or more of the owner's residences. The images could have been painted directly on the walls, but then they would not have been portable nor would they have served as insulation against the cold. Most important, while great wall paintings in domestic settings were widely admired throughout Europe in the Middle Ages, they did not have the status of woven tapestries. Hangings as rich as these, shining with brilliant silks, wools, gold, and silver, made it clear to any viewer that their owner was a person of wealth and consequence.

The kind of fabric that forms the substance of the unicorn tapestries was woven in great quantities as an industrial product during the Middle Ages and later. Today, hangings of this kind are still produced industrially in a number of highly capitalized hand-weaving factories, such as the Gobelins, Beauvais, and Aubusson in France, among others. On the other hand, there are numbers of smaller, independent tapestry-weaving shops in various parts of the world. But since wall hangings of this great size are not widely used in domestic interiors today, most people have no opportunity to live with and study the fabric intimately.

As one draws close to the unicorn tapestries (or any other tapestry-woven hangings), one sees immediately that the picture represented on the surface is not painted. Indeed the image looks like, and is, a kind of mosaic made of tiny dots of yarn that cover the surface completely. However, painted hangings imitating tapestries were commonly made in the past. Some were frankly made to serve in place of the much more expensive tapestry-woven hangings. To make them look like the real thing from a distance, the painter would use a fabric with a pronounced horizontal rib to suggest the ribbed texture that is characteristic of

Figure 57. The Start of the Hunt, *detail of Figure 16*

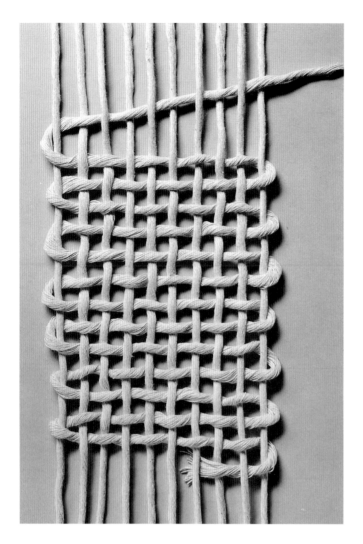

true tapestry weave. Other painted wall hangings originally served as the cartoons, or full-size patterns, that tapestry weavers followed as they built up their fabric. This practice was fairly common in the Middle Ages, and we have some references to the fact that such cartoons were hung in churches most of the year in order to save the precious woven tapestries, which would be brought out only on feast days.

It is equally clear, at close range, that the *Hunt of the Unicorn* tapestries are not needle-worked fabrics either. Large embroidered wall hangings were indeed produced in the Middle Ages and for centuries afterward, right into our own time. The basic difference between the two kinds of fabrics is this. An artisan producing a needle-worked hanging begins with a fully formed fabric whose surface is blank. The pattern (the picture that the hanging will eventually show) is built up on this preexisting fabric with needle stitches. Before the advent of synthetic yarns in modern times, the embroidery yarns were spun primarily of wool, silk, or linen fibers. In the most sumptuous needle-worked hangings the worker also used metallic yarns, which were made by twisting a flat, narrow, silver or gilt wire (tinsel) around a core yarn of white silk (to heighten the silver color) or yellow silk (for gold yarns).

From a distance, an embroidered hanging looks very much like a tapestry-woven one, because both have patterns created by an arrangement of colored (and occasionally metallic) yarns. But the two kinds of surfaces are, in fact, very different. The surface of a needle-worked hanging shows the separate stitches very clearly, the yarns varying in length and direction according to how the needle was worked into the preexisting fabric. On the other hand, the surface of a tapestry-woven hanging shows a strictly ordered series of pattern yarns, which run in one direction only, at right angles to the warp yarns around which they are woven. In tapestry weaving this interaction of the warp yarns and the pattern yarns creates the fabric and the pattern simultaneously. The one cannot exist without the other.

The tapestry weaver uses a variation of the same basic weave that a cloth weaver uses, that is, plain or tabby weave, the weave we commonly see in sheets or shirting material. The weft yarn, wound on a bobbin and carried in the weaver's hand, is interwoven with the warp yarns, which are fixed in place on the loom rather like the strings of a harp. The intersections occur at right angles to the warp, the weft yarn passing over one warp yarn, under the next, over the next, and so on, passing completely across the warp until a fabric is built up (Figure 58). The two sets of yarns have the same diameter and weight, and so the resulting fabric is smooth and even. However, in tapestry weaving the weft yarns are much finer than the warp yarns and they are packed down tightly on them, thus creating a ribbed effect (Figure 59). But more important than that, the wefts in tapestry weaving do not always pass completely across the width of the warp. Each weft is a different color from its neighbor,

and each interweaves with the warp only in that place where its color is required to form the pattern in the cartoon. Each patch of interwoven weft is like a piece in a jigsaw puzzle held in place not by the shape of its edges but by the underlying warp yarns. Since there is only one warp and one set of weft yarns, a tapestry fabric that has been finished as neatly on the back as the front is therefore reversible, the pattern showing on the back as well as the front but of course in reverse on the back (Figure 60).

Tapestries are in fact woven from the back—that is, with the weaver facing the back of the fabric—whether they are constructed on a vertical (high warp) or horizontal (low warp) loom. In the two pertinent inventories (1680 and 1728) of the de La Rochefoucauld family tapestries, the hangings are described as *haute lisse*, or high-warp, pieces. That term may also have

Opposite left: Figure 58. Yarn model of the structure of plain or tabby weave. In this illustration the warp runs vertically, and the continuous weft yarn interweaves with the warp, passing completely across the warp from one side to the other.

Opposite right: Figure 59. Yarn model of the structure of tapestry weave. Here, too, the warp runs vertically. The weft yarns of each color are interwoven with the warp in tabby binding only where the patterns call for that color. The weft yarns, much finer than the warp yarns and packed tightly together, completely cover the warp. This creates the ribbed effect characteristic of tapestry weave.

Overleaf: Figure 60. Front and back of the same section of a tapestry of The Annunciation. Southern Netherlands, 1460–80. Wool warp; wool and silk wefts. Height 3 feet, 3½ inches; width 6 feet, 11 inches (10.03 x 21.08 meters). The Metropolitan Museum of Art, The Cloisters Collection, 1971 (1971.135)

been used generically to designate tapestry-woven hangings as opposed to hangings of other kinds, and it has also been suggested that in the late Middle Ages *haute lisse* might have been used as a term signifying high quality, as haute couture is used today to signify fine clothing.

Figure 61. View of a weaver working at a low-warp loom. She sits before the front beam and passes a bobbin through the shed, which separates the odd-numbered warp yarns from the even, thus allowing the weft to pass over one set and under the other. The cartoon, or design, lies on the shelf in front of the beam and under the warp. The heddles, which control the odd and even yarns, and the mechanism that activates them by means of pedals, are visible below the warp, left of center in this view. (Photograph by Yves Debraine)

I believe that the *Hunt of the Unicorn* hangings, like other late-medieval tapestries that show such fine detail, may have been woven on horizontal looms. And so I will discuss that method briefly here. The warp, which consists of a heavy woolen yarn wound back and forth between the two beams of the loom, lies in a horizontal plane. The weaver sits before the front beam and works away from it toward the back of the loom (Figure 61). The bit of the cartoon that is being worked on lies on a board set beneath the warp yarns. The weaver can see it bit by bit in the spaces between adjacent warp yarns. By pressing alternately on a set of pedals beneath the loom, the weaver can separate the odd warp

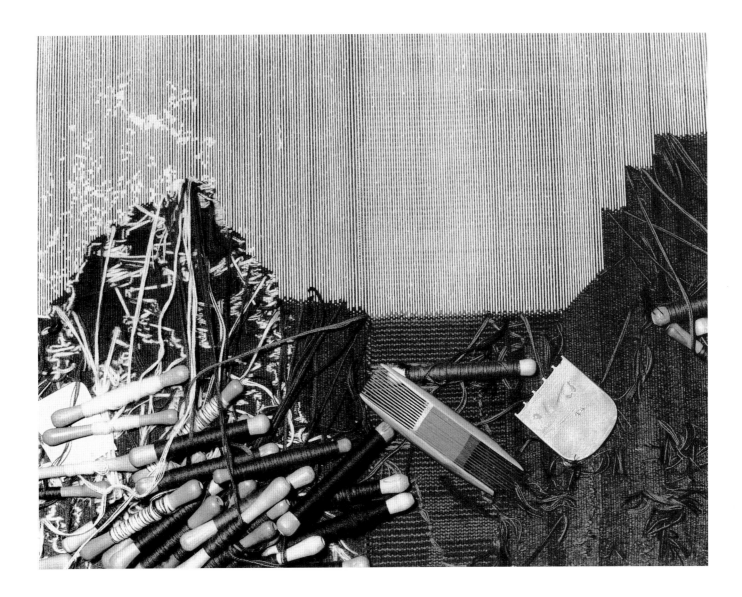

yarns from the even ones and thus create an opening or shed through which to pass the bobbins carrying the weft yarns. In this way the weft yarns pass over warp yarns 1, 3, 5, and so on, and under 2, 4, 6. The weaver, following the pattern in the cartoon and using the bobbins carrying the required color in the proper place, builds up the pattern of the finished tapestry. But the weaver sees the growing fabric only from the back (Figure 62). He or she can get glimpses of the front surface by inserting a small mirror between the cartoon and the underside of the growing web and peeking into it between the warp yarns. The weaver sees the whole front of the fabric only when the work is taken off the loom.

The weaver also has to build up the pattern on its side. For a number of technical as well as aesthetic reasons, these tapestries were planned to hang with the warp running horizontally. Therefore, the vertical axis of the pattern runs at right angles to the warp. Consequently, the weaver developed the pattern sideways, from left to right, rather than from bottom to top.

Figure 62. View of the back of a tapestry in the process of being woven on a low-warp, or horizontal, loom. The bobbins wound with weft yarns of the colors required by the pattern rest on the fabric when they are not being used. The long comb is used to press the newly laid weft yarn tightly against the completed fabric. (Photograph by Yves Debraine)

the fabric (Figure 63). A tapestry that is to be fifteen feet high would thus require five or six weavers working side by side across a loom that is somewhat more than fifteen feet long.

Obviously, only weavers having the most highly developed and refined skills were capable of weaving tapestries of this excellent quality. They had recourse to a collection of technical procedures that derived from the procedures that their painter colleagues were using at the same time. For example, while tapestry weavers could not literally shade one color into an adjacent one, they could achieve an analogous effect by means of hatching, or creating passages that resemble the interlocked teeth of combs, which, viewed from a distance, give the impression of shaded tones (Figure 64). A more subtle and difficult technique, one that the weavers of *The Hunt of the Unicorn* used to great advantage, involved the purposeful use of the tiny slits that occur as a matter of course in the weave where dissimilar adjacent tones meet, or that can be deliberately created in monochromatic passages to cast lines of subtle shadows that simulate drawing (Figure 66).

The weave is full of these and other subtleties that set *The Hunt of the Unicorn* apart from and above most other tapestries that have survived from this period. Given the fact that tapestry allows the weaver no way to create truly curved lines, then the multitude of fine, apparently effortlessly curving lines in the representation of facial features, hair, plant tendrils, and even more delicate parts of the flora must be counted

Tapestry weaving is a sensitive team endeavor. Since a weaver could work efficiently on a section of fabric only a bit wider than the distance between the hands held more or less in front of the shoulders, it is necessary for several weavers to work side by side and, simultaneously, to build up the full width (ultimately the full height) of

Above: Figure 63. View of four weavers working side by side at a low warp tapestry loom (Photograph by Yves Debraine)

Opposite: Figure 64. Detail of a medieval tapestry in The Metropolitan Museum of Art showing how the light and dark weft colors appear to shade into each other by virtue of hatching, a method that causes neighboring color areas to interpenetrate at their edges like the teeth of two combs brought together

as small miracles. But perhaps the most extraordinary technical achievement appears in the passages representing velvet garments, where, just as in nature, one sees light reflected on the edges of the forms, and between them, the deepest darks where one looks straight into the depth of the pile. In these areas the cartoon painter and weaver get the same magic realism that panel painters achieved by using oil glazes over underpainting. The unicorn tapestries are unique in this regard: there simply are no other tapestries of the period that can duplicate this extraordinary effect.

It was the designer, and perhaps also the cartoon painter (if the two were not the same person), who shares credit with the weavers for the superb quality of these tapestries. His name is not known, but it is believed that he was a painter working in Paris in the last quarter of the fifteenth

century. His work reflects the extraordinarily homogeneous and prolific artistic production coming out of Paris workshops at this time—manuscript illustrations, stained-glass windows, woodcuts, easel paintings, other tapestries. It has been suggested that the unifying influence that gives all these works a strong family resemblance was the example of a particular artist called the Coëtivy Master, who has

Above: Figure 65. Preliminary pen-and-wash drawing of the first subject in the Trojan War *tapestries,* The Mission of Antenor and the Apple of Discord. *Attributed to the Coëtivy Master, about 1460–65. Paris, Musée du Louvre, Cabinet des Dessins*

Opposite: Figure 66. Detail of a medieval tapestry in The Metropolitan Museum of Art. The small slits deliberately created by the weaver cast a line of shadows that create contours in a monochromatic area without the use of darker weft yarns.

been credited with the design of the great *Trojan War* tapestry cycle that was woven many times during the last half of the fifteenth century (Figure 65). One of the characteristic mannerisms that permeates this work turns up in the facial types of the most aggressive and hateful of the unicorn hunters. They all have long sharp noses, squinting eyes, and toothless jaws. This cohesive style spread primarily through the printed-book illustrations that appeared in great number in Paris toward the end of the fifteenth century (Figure 53). For all their originality, these artists, like many others before and after them, occasionally used

Figure 67. The Visit of the Gypsies. *Tapestry, Southern Netherlands, about 1500–1510. Manchester, New Hampshire, Currier Gallery of Art, Currier Funds* 1937.7

pattern books or sheets showing particular figure motifs that were repeated in different contexts. In *The Hunt of the Unicorn* there are three examples of this practice. First, the hand and arm of the woman caressing the unicorn's neck in one of the two fragmentary tapestries (Figure 32) repeat in reverse the hand, arm, and neck in the *Sight* piece of the *Lady with the Unicorn* tapestries in Paris (Figure 69). Also, the figure of a boy playing with his dog in the lower right corner of *The Unicorn Is Killed* (Figure 13) was taken from the pattern that served for the same detail in one of the late-fifteenth-century *Trojan War* tapestries (Figure 65). The figures of the lord and lady standing to the left of the boy in the same unicorn tapestry appear again in similar but not precisely the same form in the right foreground of a tapestry showing gypsies visiting a castle (Figure 67).

Despite the fact that this designer seems to have borrowed a few details from existing sources, there can be no doubt that the seven *Hunt of the Unicorn* tapestries were commissioned and designed to order and not made as pieces for a dealer's stock. Late-medieval tapestries of this high quality were created at the behest of either a superior entrepreneur-merchant or an individual of enormous wealth. The method of producing such hangings was simple enough, but it required great expertise on everyone's part and vast amounts of capital. The person responsible for the commission specified the subject of the series of tapestries and then chose an artist to create the original designs and possibly also the full-size cartoons that the weavers would work from. All of this was done by contract. Then the producer (whether or not he was also the patron of the project) arranged for the materials to be chosen and purchased and for the artisans to be engaged. He saw to it that payments for materials, labor, and shop expenses would be made as the contract specified. He also supervised the work to completion and arranged for the delivery of the tapestries to the patron. If that patron was not a merchant-producer but a private individual, he might retrieve the cartoons from the designer so that no other editions could be woven. On the other hand, a merchant-producer who paid for the artwork would keep the cartoons and make other editions for other patrons.

The entire process was an industrial operation executed according to the highest standards. That sounds odd to modern ears only because the idea of the artist-craftsman, an individual who both designs and makes the work of art, is more familiar to us today than the notion that fine works of art can be produced, and in the past commonly were produced, through industrial teamwork.

Some years before the *Hunt of the Unicorn* tapestries were made, people like Pasquier Grenier, a renowned tapestry, grain, and wine merchant of Tournai, and Philip the Good of Burgundy caused bespoken tapestries to be designed and produced. The most celebrated entrepreneur of the late fifteenth and early sixteenth century (when these tapestries were produced), known today is Pieter van Aelst, who operated in Brussels. He served as tapestry specialist to Philip the Fair of Austria and to the Holy See. It was van Aelst who had the *Acts of the Apostles* tapestries woven for the Sistine Chapel after designs by Raphael and his school. Van Aelst's reputation for producing tapestries of only the highest quality enhanced the reputation for superior products that Brussels already enjoyed, with the result that specialists today tend to attribute to the looms of Brussels all the richest and aesthetically superior tapestries that have survived from the end of the fifteenth and early sixteenth centuries. It is perfectly possible that the seven hangings in *The Hunt of the Unicorn* were designed and woven under the direction of a producer established in Brussels; but there is no internal or external evidence to confirm or deny that idea.

An Appreciation

From this discussion of the technical and industrial nature of tapestry weaving, it should be apparent that in order to appreciate the quality of such a work of art one must look at its *substance*, the fabric itself, as well as at the image it displays; for these are not paintings. In a way they are more like stained-glass panels, which also depend on a medium that has very particular qualities that differ from the qualities of paint. A few of the remarkable technical details in these seven hangings have already been mentioned: the fluid curves of fine lines; the clever use of slits instead of expressed lines to define the drawing in certain monochromatic areas; and the magic realism in the depictions of cut velvet. These bespeak master craftsmanship.

Furthermore, few of even the finest tapestries that have survived from the period around 1500 show the brilliant and extraordinarily varied colors that we see in *The Hunt of the Unicorn*. There are pinks and soft yellows and greens and oranges that rarely appear in other late-medieval tapestries. This is due in part to the exceptionally fine state of preservation that the tapestries enjoy, but perhaps even more to the excellent quality of the dyes that were used to color the pattern yarns. The same may be said of the silver and gilt yarns that are used lavishly in each of the seven hangings: they are of the finest quality and they are well preserved.

As for the high quality of the design, it is enough to call attention to the refinement in the depiction of all the flora and the startling expression of specific personalities and psychological states in the faces of all the characters including the unicorn itself. This is rare in tapestries that have survived from this period. But it is here and it proves, if there ever was any question about it, that the best tapestries are, on their own terms, equal to the best paintings.

Opposite: Figure 68. The Unicorn Leaps out of the Stream, *detail of Figure 40*

Figure 69. Sight, *from* The Lady with the Unicorn. *Tapestry,*
Southern Netherlands, 1480–90. Height 10 feet, 2¼ inches; width
10 feet, 9⅞ inches (3.10 x 3.30 meters). Paris, Musée du Moyen-Age, Cluny

Opposite: Figure 70. Hearing, *from* The Lady with the Unicorn.
Tapestry, Southern Netherlands, 1480–90. Height 12 feet, 1¼ inches;
width 9 feet, 6⅛ inches (3.69 x 2.90 meters). Paris, Musée du Moyen-Age, Cluny

Figure 71. Taste, *from* The Lady with the Unicorn. *Tapestry, Southern Netherlands, 1480–90. Height 12 feet, 3½ inches; width 15 feet, 1⅞ inches (3.75 x 4.62 meters). Paris, Musée du Moyen-Age, Cluny*

Opposite: Figure 72. Smell, *from* The Lady with the Unicorn. *Tapestry, Southern Netherlands, 1480–90. Height 12 feet, ⅞ inch; width 10 feet, 6 inches (3.68 x 3.20 meters). Paris, Musée du Moyen-Age, Cluny*

It is meaningless to compare *The Hunt of the Unicorn* to the six pieces of *The Lady with the Unicorn* in the Musée de Cluny in Paris (Figures 69–74) in terms of quality. It is like comparing apples and oranges. Both groups of tapestries are equally beautiful, supremely well designed, and extremely well made. But they are completely different from one another. The only thing they have in common is the presence of the uni-

corn and the fact that they both represent the most refined French court taste at the end of the fifteenth century. The tapestries in Paris were woven in the 1480s, some ten to fifteen years earlier than *The Hunt of the Unicorn*. The mood of their compositions is serene and monumental, the opposite of the dynamic spirit in all the Cloisters tapestries except the fragments from *The Mystic Hunt of the Unicorn* and *The Unicorn in*

Captivity. The millefleur backgrounds of the latter and its companion, *The Start of the Hunt*, where whole plants crowd together as they grow out of the ground, differ from the Paris backgrounds, which are more sparsely scattered with plants that have been uprooted and cut at the bottom of their stalks.

Both groups of tapestries have enigmatic subjects. I have attempted here to interpret the unicorn-hunting tapestries as best I can in the light of our present knowledge, but there are still some unanswered questions. The same is true of *The Lady with the Unicorn.* Traditional wisdom suggests that the five ladies with their different attributes represent the five senses. Various interpretations—none of them accepted unanimously—have been offered for the sixth piece, which shows a lady standing before a tent with a valance that bears the inscription

Above: Figure 73. A Mon Seul Desir *(interpretation uncertain) from* The Lady with the Unicorn. *Tapestry, Southern Netherlands, 1480–90. Height 12 feet, 2½ inches; width 15 feet, 4½ inches (3.72 x 4.68 meters). Paris, Musée du Moyen-Age, Cluny*

Opposite: Figure 74. Touch, *from* The Lady with the Unicorn. *Tapestry, Southern Netherlands, 1480–90. Height 12 feet, 2¹⁄₁₆ inches; width 11 feet, 7¾ inches (3.71 x 3.55 meters). Paris, Musée du Moyen-Age, Cluny*

"A Mon Seul Desir." The six tapestries have also been construed in many other ways. Recently it has been suggested that *The Lady with the Unicorn* is in fact a romance, a version of *The Hunt of the Unicorn as Lover*.

On the other hand, there are certain similarities in the history of the tapestries in The Cloisters and at the Musée de Cluny that suggest avenues of inquiry that may lead to new facts concerning the former. The pieces now in Paris were known in the region of the château de Boussac in the eighteenth century, but it was not until the writer Prosper Mérimée saw them in 1841 and became concerned about their condition that the Commission des Monuments Historiques became involved in their preservation. Meanwhile, George Sand's husband and son saw the hangings in the château de Boussac in 1835, not far from her house in the country, and brought them to her attention. She then became seriously interested in the hangings and began to give them publicity. In 1847 she wrote an article about them, illustrated with engravings after drawings by her son, Maurice. She promoted the tapestries again in print, somewhat fancifully, in 1862 and 1871. Finally, through the intervention of the Commission des Monuments Historiques, the nation bought *The Lady with the Unicorn* in 1882 to hang in the Musée des Thermes at the Hôtel de Cluny in Paris.

George Sand was convinced at one point that she had seen two more tapestries in the set, that is, a total of eight pieces. But drawings made in 1842 of the installation in the château de Boussac indicated that there were never more than six *Lady with the Unicorn* tapestries there. Nevertheless, we know that Jean IV le Viste, whose arms appear blazoned on banners in all six of the pieces in Paris, owned thirteen other tapestries that showed unicorns, beasts, sibyls, and his coat of arms on red grounds. They are lost, but they appear in an inventory taken in 1595 in the château de Montaigu-le-Blin in the Bourbonnais. Is it so strange, then, to imagine that the unidentified patron AE also commissioned other unicorn tapestries, at least three sets of them, all marked with his (or their) cipher, and that some of the hangings are lost? We also know that the *Lady with the Unicorn* hangings probably went to the château de Boussac in 1660 through the marriage of Jeanne de la Roche Ayman, one of Jean IV le Viste's distant heirs, to François de Rilhac, owner of the château de Boussac. Should we not, then, take a leaf from this book and stop looking fruitlessly for the patron AE among the members of the de La Rochefoucauld family who were living around 1500 and search instead for the owner of the coat of arms depicted on the collar of the greyhound in *The Start of the Hunt* (Figure 75)? Like Jean IV le Viste, he (or they) may have had heirs who took property with them when they married into another family living in another place.

Opposite: Figure 75. The Start of the Hunt, *detail of Figure 16*

Appendix I: Flora in the Unicorn Tapestries

The following is adapted from an article by E. J. Alexander and Carol H. Woodward, with drawings by Walter Graham, originally published by the New York Botanical Garden in 1941 and reprinted numerous times since then. The tapestries are referred to in the order in which they were originally thought to be placed; titles and figure numbers used in the primary text of this book have been inserted for the reader's convenience.

A Contribution to Art

Each science and every art is dependent on one or more others for its complete understanding. Botany, for example, frequently turns to geology, and art often calls upon one of the sciences for an interpretation.

This essay is the result of the New York Botanical Garden's study of the flora of these hangings, which are owned by The Metropolitan Museum of Art. Through identification of a large proportion of the plants, new light has been thrown on the tapestries, on the people of the day, and on their knowledge and culture. New questions have arisen as to who these designers and weavers were who had such an intimate acquaintance with plants that they were able to reproduce details of leaf and flower with a perfection unparalleled in any other art form of the period. How many artisans of today could match them in botanical knowledge? They even carefully placed the moisture-loving plants at the water's edge, the correct forest trees together, and the plants of open spaces generally where they belonged in nature. As artisans they were evidently excellent ecologists. A study of botanical illustration of the late fifteenth and early sixteenth centuries makes it plain that men who posed as connoisseurs of plants in that day drew but crudely in comparison with those unknown folk who labored on the tapestries.

Acquaintance with the flora in *The Hunt of the Unicorn* increases our admiration for these artisans of long ago and adds to the impressiveness of the tapestries themselves. Science, which is the search for truth, has in this instance contributed toward the appreciation of a masterpiece of art.

The Flora of the Unicorn Tapestries: The Woven Portrayal of the Legendary and Symbolic Hunt of the Unicorn

At The Cloisters in Fort Tryon Park, New York City, hangs one of the most remarkable sets of medieval tapestries in existence anywhere in the world today. Although because of their subject the seven hangings have been compared with the famous unicorn tapestries in the Cluny Museum of Paris, they are unique, distinct in design from their Paris contemporaries, and more realistic in treatment. They are virtually incomparable in their grandeur of design, in the quality of the weaving, the subtlety and variety of their coloring, and the brilliance of their dyes today, despite the vicissitudes they have encountered through the centuries. They are noteworthy also for the accuracy of the plants and animals which form a dominant part of the setting of each piece. Except for minor repairs six of the tapestries are intact. Two fragments are all that remain of a seventh tapestry in the series.

For centuries they remained in the Rochefoucauld chateau at Verteuil. Shortly after 1920 they were acquired by John D. Rockefeller Jr., who presented them in 1938 to The Metropolitan Museum of Art for The Cloisters, where many of the plants depicted are now being grown.

There are approximately 101 different kinds of plants represented in the six large tapestries and the fragments. About 85 percent of these are identifiable. The others remain, on the whole, complete mysteries. An attempt is made here to point out some of the conspicuous plants and to discuss some of the controversial ones from the standpoint of their actual resemblance to plants that are known to grow wild in the region from which the tapestries came or to have been cultivated at that early date in western Europe. The botanical outlook will often conflict with the symbolical, which has been so ably set forth by Mrs. Allan Marquand [Eleanor C. Marquand, "Plant Symbolism in the Unicorn Tapestries," *Parnassus*, 10, no. 5 (October

Opposite: Figure 76. The Unicorn Is Found, detail of Figure 34

1938), pp. 3–8, 33, 40]. But even with a frequently divergent outlook, Mrs. Marquand's success in giving names to 46 of the plants has been an inspiration and often a guide in the present work, although this study has been made entirely independent of hers. While some of her names have provided clues, others have been merely provocative. The religious and secular symbolism with which she deals have been thrust aside here in favor of the botanical point of view. The accuracy of the drawing of the majority of the plants has induced the use of resemblance rather than symbolism as a guide where our ideas have differed from hers.

Even upon casual examination of the tapestries, one is immediately impressed with the striking difference in design and execution of the first and last of the series as contrasted with the others. In these two the plants are scattered over the entire background in a millefleurs pattern, while in the others they appear to grow in naturalistic manner, creating the impression of a scene at the edge of the woods, with forest trees in the rear, flowers of field and open woodland at the front, and small trees and shrubs between. In these the representations are on the whole more accurate and less stylized, though more than 40 of the 53 plants in the first and seventh tapestries [*The Start of the Hunt,* Figure 16, and *The Unicorn in Captivity,* Figure 23] are recognizable. However, one is led to the conclusion that the designer of these tapestries was not always familiar with the plants as they grew, and that he depended on memory or hearsay for their form. Or, he may have been less of a naturalistic artist than a producer of patterns, hence he converted the plants into the style of semi-formal design that was his forte.

In initiating a study of the flora of the tapestries, we had hoped that identification of the plants might furnish a clue as to where the tapestries had been woven. But this idea had to be discarded early, first because the plants depicted are nearly all widespread in western Europe, thus preventing the narrowing down to any one area, and second, because of the realization that the designer may have come from a different country and used the plants which he knew rather than those that were growing in the region of the weavers.

The first and seventh tapestries have by far the greatest number of plants in them, and in view of their similarity of design and floral content they are best discussed before the middle group is considered.

Next to the figures in the first, and the unicorn in the seventh, the outstanding feature in each is the tree which forms the central focus. It is a strange-looking tree which catches the eye in the seventh tapestry, with flat rosettes of pointed leaves at the ends of the branches and a big red-orange fruit set in the center of each. It resembles no tree on earth, but the fruit is a perfect pomegranate, offering an excellent example of how a designer tried to cope with a subject with which he was only half familiar. The pomegranate tree not being hardy in western Europe, he could scarcely have known it unless he had traveled widely, but its fruits he no doubt had frequently seen, for they were brought in by eastern traders from the earliest times.

The central tree in the first tapestry is, in our opinion, the common cherry, *Prunus avium.* This was considered by Mrs. Marquand as the rowan tree, her conclusion presumably based as much on the symbolism and power attached to this plant as on the small red fruits and the narrow, compound-looking leaves. There have consequently been many discussions about the identity of this tree, as well as another so-called rowan to its right, but the rowan, or European mountain-ash, like ours, has terminal clusters containing many berries, whereas the cherry bears its fruits either singly or in small clusters on old wood somewhat back from the tips of the branches, exactly as they are shown in the tapestry. Because the pomegranate in No. 7 was stylized she has thought that this was too, but the argument does not hold, because the artist had obviously never seen a pomegranate tree, while both cherry and rowan would have been well known to him, and it does not seem, in view of other accuracies, that any designer would have gone so far out of his way as to stylize a familiar tree out of all semblance to its natural habit.

Over at the edge of the forest in No. 1 is the other tree which has been called a rowan. It is similar to the cherry but has larger fruits which appear white but at close range are seen to be pale blue. This we believe to be a plum, which is a tree of the forest's edge, while the cherry is a tree of more open ground, as it is shown here. It is especially notable that the fruits have been made larger than the cherries and are shown without stems, thus still further suggesting blue plums.

Back of the spear-point of the foremost huntsman is a small misty yellowish tree which by most francophiles is thought to be a mimosa (*Acacia*). But it could not be, for the mimosas of France have come from Australia, and Australia was not discovered by Europeans until the seventeenth century. What is more likely is that this is a distant cluster of elms with reflected sunlight producing the yellowish effect. The remaining forest trees are recognized clearly as oak, linden, aspen, and walnut.

Two unusual-looking plants are the palm-like ones in front of the dogs. At first glance, they seem to be ferns, but one soon realizes that there are no ferns of this type in Europe. They are apparently young date palms, small plants raised indoors from the seeds of dates that had been shipped in from the East.

Of the conspicuous flowers which occur only in the first tapestry there are but two. One is the white thistle, the other a hawkweed of undetermined species. In the seventh tapestry, however, there are a number of flowers which appear there alone. Among them are two exquisitely woven carnations (*Dianthus caryophyllus*), their curling leaves and toothed petals and the long branched style extending out from the center of each flower being as finely done as an etching. In each of the other tapestries (except the fragments) there are other species of *Dianthus*, commonly known as pinks, their broad leaves indicating that they were intended for *Dianthus seguieri*, as most of the other European pinks (such as *D. plumarius*) have grass-like leaves. Also conspicuous in the seventh is the Madonna lily (*Lilium candidum*)—which is not the same as our Easter lily. Less noticeable but of certain determination once it is found is the bistort (*Polygonum Bistorta*); also the common cuckoo-pint (*Arum Maculatum*), a plant which takes the

place of our jack-in-the-pulpit in woodlands of England and the continent. The spurred blue flowers of columbine (*Aquilegia vulgaris*) are at the bottom near the center and at the left near the top. A wild orchid, possibly *Orchis mascula*, appears immediately in front of the unicorn, its stalk of flowers barely visible against his white body.

A unique flower (or fruit) in the seventh tapestry has proved annoyingly intriguing. It is a plant of rosette growth with stalks bearing peculiarly drooping structures, each like a saucer held on edge with battlemented borders, the "saucer" attached in one case near the center, in another near the top. This same thing appears in fragmentary form but a different color in the first, but both are completely unidentifiable. It is one of several small plants to which no clue can be found.

Two especially prominent flowers appear in the first and seventh tapestries without being shown in any of the others. A yellow daisy-like flower with smaller heads and more numerous rays than the other daisies is evidently *Inula salicifolia*, a relative of the elecampane of gardens. Appearing as an original in the seventh and on the restoration in the first is the milk or holy thistle, *Silybum Marianum*, clearly recognized by the light veining on its leaves and the leafy bracts at the base of the flower-head. Although native to the Mediterranean region, it has long been spread over Europe as a weed.

At the lower right edge of Tapestry No. 7 is one of the most perfectly and beautifully depicted flowers in the entire series, even though only half a plant is represented. It is the common dandelion, *Taraxacum officinale*.

Many of the flowers in these two tapestries are easily recognized. Some of them occur in slightly different form throughout the series. To speak of some of the more conspicuous among them, the English bluebell (*Scilla nonscripta*) is one of the most frequently repeated, occurring in blue, pink, yellow, and white, sometimes in flower, often as not in fruit of equally varying color. The English daisy (*Bellis perennis*) is almost as frequently shown, in white, pink, and yellow, but always in such distinctly characteristic form of flower and leaf as to indicate that the color was varied merely for effect.

Two types of viola are represented with colors

corresponding to those of the scilla. It seems reasonable to believe that all of those with rounded leaves are intended, despite their hues, for the sweet violet, *Viola odorata*. Those with long leaves toothed in various fashions and with flowers borne on leafy stems are thus plainly intended to represent the pansy (*Viola tricolor*), which even in the wild state occurs in numerous combinations of color and with considerable variance both in the width and in the toothing of the leaves.

Strawberries, shown with both flowers and fruits, are beautifully drawn. The narcissi are equally perfect, always in yellow and unmistakable. Their fruits, seldom observed in gardens, are shown in light blue, perhaps to represent the glaucous bloom which covers the pods. Most of them have the characteristic pear shape, but some, even on the same plant, are curiously elongate. This may have been done for the purpose of filling small spaces to better advantage of balance.

The primroses represented in the first and seventh tapestries are all shown with yellow or orange flowers, while some of those in the other four large panels are of pink or red. Since the primroses with reddish tones are all high mountain species, and only lowland plants seem to be depicted in the tapestries, one must again allow for artist's license or assume that the designer was a traveled man who indicated here colors that he had seen in other regions.

The periwinkle (*Vinca*) is easily identifiable as it appears only in the two normal colors of white and blue, always with opposite leaves, and in 1 and 7 (not elsewhere) with a pair of terminal tendril coils. These tendrils do not belong on the plant, but it must be supposed that they were placed there to indicate that the vinca grows like a vine—though it is more properly a creeper.

The white campion (*Lychnis alba*), whose untoothed opposite leaves and white flowers make it easily distinguished, is recognized in several of the tapestries.

There are a number of plants of the Mustard family (*Cruciferae*) represented in all of the hangings. Some of them in Tapestries 2, 3, 4, and 6—the smaller ones with red, orange, or yellow flowers—cannot be positively placed except as to

family. The others—that is, the larger ones—are more definite. As stocks (*Mathiola incana*) and wallflowers (*Cheiranthus cheiri*) they are among the most conspicuous of flowers in all the series. In the weaving they look much alike, but the stocks have slightly larger flowers in white, pink, and pinkish red, and leaves more blunt-tipped and "floppy" and a bit more bluish green, while the wallflowers are in yellow, orange, and orange-red and have leaves somewhat pointed and stiff and more definitely green. The two blue-flowered crucifers, both shown with toothed leaves, are more clearly distinguishable. The dame's rocket or dame's violet (*Hesperis matronalis*) has taller stems, narrower, longer leaves, and much larger flowers than the other, which is apparently honesty (*Lunaria*) with small flowers on short spikes and with much broader leaves. In nature, both are purplish in hue instead of blue.

A study of the background of the four hangings which follow the first one on the long wall in the tapestry hall gives one a glimpse of the edge of a typical forest in western Europe, for here are the oak, the elm, the holly, another tree which is probably a beech, and in front of these, smaller trees and shrubs.

The holly is easily recognized by its red berries and spiny leaves; the oak by the characteristic shape of its leaves, some of which are spotted with reddish galls. In the elm the foliage is indistinct, but the shape of the tree is unmistakable for, though the branches are more stiff, they have an upward sweep not unlike that of the American elm. The fourth tree has been a puzzling one throughout this study, for its glossy-appearing oval leaves have not been confined to this subject alone. Out of the many suggestions made, our decision to call it a beech was based mainly on its natural prevalence among oaks and elms in a forest, though we were guided somewhat by the weaver's implication of smooth bark. In the fourth tapestry [*The Unicorn at Bay*, Figure 44] one of these trees has just been cut down, perhaps to be fashioned into a staff.

All of the tapestries except the second [*The Unicorn Is Found*, Figure 34] and sixth [*The Unicorn Is Killed and Brought to the Castle*, Figure

The Start of the Hunt—*First of the Seven Unicorn Tapestries*

The background trees of cherry, oak, linden, plum, aspen, and walnut are easily seen. Two or three seedling date palms are conspicuous toward the foreground at the right. Among the thirty to thirty-five different kinds of plants which appear in the millefleurs background of this hanging, the narcissus, vinca, English daisy, violet, strawberry, and English bluebell (Scilla) stand out prominently.

50] have a tree as the central feature, and in each a different kind is shown. In the third it is an oak (*Quercus robur*, as undoubtedly are the rest), and to its left appears the first new tree in the forest scene. The large blue-black fruits indicate that it is the bullace plum, *Prunus domestica* var. *Institia*.

In Tapestry No. 4 [*The Unicorn at Bay*, Figure 44] the central tree is unmistakably an orange, easily recognized here, as it is in the lower right corner of No. 2, by its winged petioles (leaf-stalks) and the presence of flowers and fruits on the branches at the same time. To the right of the central orange is a walnut tree well laden with large brown nuts. Beside it, bearing small red fruits, is a tree that has been a problem, for it does not fit into any forest scheme of the region concerned. We are therefore inclined to accept Mrs. Marquand's suggestion that it is a strawberry tree (*Arbutus unedo*). While extremely rare in the wild on the European continent, it has been cultivated there for so many centuries that the designers could easily have considered it familiar enough to be included among the forest trees.

In the upper right-hand corner of this same tapestry is a tree with richly colored fruit that is probably an apricot.

One of the two fragments of the fifth tapestry [*The Mystic Hunt of the Unicorn*, Figure 27], which hang above the door, contains the only apple tree shown in the series. This was the central feature of the original tapestry and was identified by Mrs. Marquand as a pomegranate, but a comparison with the pomegranates in the two other tapestries (3 and 7) reveals a totally different structure of the fruit. The design of these fragments is marked by the stronger light which is thrown against the figures, and in the original this brightness was brought out in the apple by the golden threads which were used to indicate highlights. The threads are now browned with age, so it is only at close range that the true form of the apple, with a prominently marked blossom end, can be distinguished. Several oaks, a holly, a branch of beech, and a few small leaves of walnut are the only other trees shown in the fragments. Most prominent is a row of red and white roses twining about the enclosure wherein the unicorn has been captured by the virgin. The only flower shown is a bit of periwinkle.

The sixth tapestry in the series [*The Unicorn Is Killed and Brought to the Castle*] again shows the forest trees to be oak, holly, beech, and elm.

The shrubs or forest undergrowth forming the middle ground and the dominant notes at the lower corners are, like the trees, quite similar throughout the four central tapestries.

Most frequently depicted is the hawthorn in full flower, exquisitely designed, and accompanied by shrubby specimens of oak and holly, one of the former bearing the typical acorns of the English oak. There are also plums, cherries, hazelnuts, and a beautiful blackberry climbing over the branches of one of the hazels. A noteworthy tree is the medlar (*Mespilus germanic*), whose fruit is almost unknown in America, though common in Europe for many centuries. It is related to the apple and is marked by a greatly enlarged blossom end. Most notable of all is the single pomegranate tree near the lower left corner of the third tapestry. Here, in contrast to the seventh hanging, the tree is correctly drawn, telling us plainly that the designer must have been familiar with it as it grew, not with its fruits alone.

The only occurrence of the peach tree is at the lower right of Tapestry No. 4, where the large grooved fruits are easily recognized. In front of the fountain in the second tapestry and below the head of the unicorn in the fourth is an old-fashioned cabbage rose of the type once widely cultivated in Europe and America, but now displaced by newer-bred forms.

Flowers—that is, herbaceous plants—appear only in the foreground of these four principal scenes of the hunt. Here we have some of the most interesting, most obvious, and some of the most difficult in the entire series to identify. Certain ones are present in all four of the scenes, foremost being the pot-marigold (*Calendula officinalis*), correctly and unmistakably drawn. Also present in Tapestries 2, 3, 4, and 6 is the wintercherry or Chinese lantern-plant (*Physalis alkekengi*), conspicuous by the bright red husks which cover its fruits. This plant, while native from the eastern Mediterranean to Japan, had been cultivated for so many centuries in Europe that it would have been as familiar a plant in that day as it is to us now in America.

Some of the plants shown reveal an acuteness of observation that is equaled only by the perfection of workmanship in the weaving. A glance at the plantains (*Plantago cornuti*) in the third and fourth tapestries, the cattails (*Typha latifolia*) in the water toward the right side of the fourth, and the feverfew (*Chrysanthemum parthenium*) near the stream in the lower left of No. 4 show both designer and worker at their best.

In the daisy-like plants, or composites, however, their eyes were more confused. There is not the differentiation that would be expected in depicting these familiar flowers of the field and open woods. However, it is quite apparent that they intended to show in the third tapestry, for example, the ox-eye or common field daisy (*Chrysanthemum Leucanthemum*), the corn-marigold (*Chrysanthemum segetum*), and a groundsel (*Senecio paludosus*).

The fourth tapestry, in which the unicorn is shown defending himself, contains a larger number of puzzling plants than any other. Several of them show only leaves, but even they are quite different in form from those seen anywhere else. Two with flowers are, however, equally conjectural, though the leaves of one indicate that it may be a thistle in bud. The other has rather broad, unindented leaves and at the tip of each branch a blob of purplish color that might be either a flower or a fruit.

In all of the hangings only three members of the mint family appear, the field mint (*Mentha arvensis*) rather inconspicuously placed in the first tapestry, the common sage (*Salvia officinalis*) prominently set against the fountain in the second, and clary (*Salvia sclarea*) centrally located near the base of the oak in the third.

At the water's edge near the lower right of the third is the yellow flag (*Iris pseudacorus*). This same iris in an orange tone appears also in the fourth. Mrs. Marquand has called these plants the yellow and orange daylilies (*Hemerocallis*) but the reflexed sepals and erect petals used elsewhere for an iris have also been used here, while lily-like flowers have been shown in their true form on the one Madonna lily. Moreover, it is very doubtful that daylilies were known in western Europe at that period.

Under the right-hand hunter in the third tapestry is an unfamiliar-looking blue flower with cut leaves. This is probably *Nigella arvensis*, which lacks the feathery involucre so familiar in our garden plant called love-in-a-mist (*Nigella damascena*). While nigella leaves are actually cut into thread-like segments, the type of weaving here necessitates the making of coarser leaves so that they will be visible. In the fourth and sixth tapestries plants of a similar design appear both with yellow and with red flowers, in one instance on the same plant. These we assume are meant for the pheasant's eye (*Adonis aestivalis*), whose flowers occur in both these colors.

Below the lower left "A" in the fourth tapestry is the only forget-me-not in the entire series.

Besides a handsome bearded iris, standing erect in the foreground, and the usual ground-cherries, pinks, primulas, pansies, violets, and campions, the sixth tapestry brings two newcomers to the scene: one the safflower (*Carthamus tinctorius*), the "scarlet thistle" of Mrs. Marquand; the other a relative of the pinks and campions, but a plant wholly unknown in America, hence without a common name here. At the top of the stem it has white flowers with cleft petals and on the lower branches enlarged calyces from which the berry-like fruits have evidently fallen. If our assumption is correct, its botanical name is *Cucubalus baccifer*.

The restorations, which are best discounted in the final analysis of plants represented, nevertheless, demand attention. The large areas woven in across the bottom of the first and seventh contain only plants depicted elsewhere in the same two tapestries. A careful survey will locate the original of the design for each plant, though the newer work is inferior and the colors are less brilliant.

The cluster of iris, for example, in the new work on No. 1 is a complete copy of the original in No. 7, even to the placing on the left-hand spray of two unnatural flowers. In addition, a butterfly on one of the iris flowers in the restored portion is clearly a copy of one on the carnation beside the iris in No. 7. The calendula which appears twice on the piece across the bottom of No. 1 and once on No. 7 seems to have no exact original, but near the lower right-hand letter, and again several plants away to the left on No. 7, appear two specimens that are obviously the same plant less conventionalized. These are probably the designer's source for the restoration. The other plants in these restorations are too easily identified to call for discussion in detail.

The patch in the lower right corner of the fifth tapestry is of little or no importance, for its inferior execution and the totally foreign nature of the plants represented are quite out of keeping with the tapestries otherwise. The picturing of the garden pea and the red pepper is interesting, however, as this is the only appearance of vegetables in the series, and here only in a patch of much later date than the original. The musk-mallow also is shown here but nowhere else.

At the left edge of the patch, below the lady's robe, the presence of the safflower, beautifully worked out but partially obliterated, makes one wish for the remainder of the original part of this corner. That longing, however, must remain forever ungratified.

The more one gazes at the original work in these superb tapestries, the more familiar flowers one discovers—and the more one marvels that a designer who could conceive the grandeur of the drama of the unicorn hunt for the weavers to reproduce could at the same time suggest the details of more than 100 kinds of flowers—most of which were reproduced with an accuracy, even a feeling for form and texture, that might well be the envy of an artist or an artisan today. Perhaps even a greater wonder is that a band of weavers could carry out to such perfection the flower petals, veins of leaves, thorns, and other such fine details, with a precision of line and color that in most of the plants is unassailable.

The unicorn tapestries at The Cloisters in New York stand alone for their magnificence, their perfection. To those of us who have closely studied the plants depicted in them, that perfection reaches its height in the flowers, shrubs, and trees. Plant illustration as shown in books of the fifteenth and sixteenth centuries was crude. In the accurate representation of plant life, the weavers' skill in these tapestries represents the highest art form of the period.

Checklist of Plants in the Unicorn Tapestries
By E. J. Alexander and Carol H. Woodward

A checklist of the plants is given here with one or more drawings of each subject shown in its relative position in the design. The numbers are for reference to the list. The drawings were made by Walter Graham, through the cooperation of The Metropolitan Museum of Art.

Changes in the identification of a few of the subjects since the original article was written, and discovery of several duplications in the original numbering, have altered the total figure to 101 different kinds of plants (including fruits of two of the flowers), of which 16 still remain complete mysteries. Of the remaining 85, the majority are unquestionable in their identity. Even though one plant, for example, which occurs several times in the second tapestry, is shown with only four petals instead of five, there can be little doubt from a study of its form that it was intended for the pimpernel. In practically every other instance, such details as the number of petals are woven into the pattern with great accuracy. Wherever there is still doubt about the identity of a plant, a question-mark is used.

As can be seen in the preceding article, color has been a determining factor in several instances, yet it has usually been backed by a distinguishing form of leaf or general growth habit. The reader who visits The Cloisters and uses this list with the drawings as a guide can readily see why, for example, No. 64 was called the ox-eye daisy and No. 62 the corn-marigold; No. 22 the wallflower and No. 26 the dame's violet.

Even a study of these drawings will reveal to some degree the difference in style of the first and seventh from the other five tapestries.

So far as possible in the next seven pages the list of plants accompanies the tapestry in which they occur.

TAPESTRY No. I
The Start of the Hunt

Tapestry No. 1

1. Scilla nonscripta (English bluebell)
2.   ?
3.   ?
4. Lunaria biennis or L. rediviva (Honesty)
5. Hieracium or Crepis (Hawkweed)
6. Narcissus (fruit) (Daffodil)
7. Prunus avium or P. cerasus (Cherry)
8. Fragaria vesca (Strawberry)
9. Ulmus procera (Elm)
10. Tilia europaea (Linden)
11. Prunus domestica (?) (Blue plum)
12. Populus tremula (Aspen)
13. Juglans regia (Walnut)
14. Narcissus pseudo-narcissus (Daffodil)
15. Sagittaria sagittifolia (Arrowhead)
16. Mentha arvensis (Mint)
17. Carex muricata (Sedge)
18. Cirsium or Carduus (White thistle)
19. Dianthus seguieri (Broad-leaved pink)
20. Hyacinthus or Scilla (Hyacinth or Squill)
21. Inula salicina (A relative of elecampane)
22. Cheiranthus cheiri (Wallflower)
23. Alchemilla vulgaris (Lady's mantle)
24.   ?
25. Viola odorata (Sweet violet)

(The list continues on page 112.)

Tapestry No. 2

The Unicorn Is Found

26. Hesperis matronalis (Dame's rocket or Dame's violet)
27.   ?
28. Vinca major or V. minor (Periwinkle)
29.   ?
30. Trifolium hybridum (Alsatian clover; Alsike)
31.   ?
32. Centaurea cyanus (Cornflower; Bachelor's button)
33. Rumex acetosa (Garden sorrel)
34. Phoenix dactylifera (Date palm)
35. Ruscus aculeatus (Butcher's broom)
36. Bellis perennis (English daisy)
37. Calendula officinalis (Pot-marigold)
38. Dianthus superbus (Fringed pink)
39.   ?

Tapestry No. 2

40. Fagus sylvatica (Beech)
41. Prunus domestica (Blue plum)
42. Mespilus germanica (Medlar)
43. Rosa centifolia (Cabbage rose)
44. Viola tricolor (Pansy)
45. Lychnis alba (White campion)
46.   ?
47. Salvia officinalis (Sage)
48. Anagallis arvensis (Pimpernel)
49.   ?
50. Physalis alkekengi (Ground-cherry; Chinese lantern-plant)
51. Citrus sinensis (Orange)

Tapestry No. 3

The Unicorn Leaps Out of the Stream

Tapestry No. 3

52. Prunus domestica var. Institia (Damson; Bullace plum)

53. Ilex aquifolium (Holly)

54. Corylus avellana (Hazelnut; Filbert)

55. Phyteuma (Rampion)

56. Adonis aestivalis (Pheasant's-eye)

57.   ?

58.   ?

59. Crataegus oxyacantha (Hawthorn)

60. Punica granatum (Pomegranate)

61. Senecio paludosus (Groundsel; Ragwort)

62. Chrysanthemum segetum (Corn-marigold)

63. Salvia sclarea (Clary)

64. Chrysanthemum leucanthemum (Ox-eye daisy;
 Common field daisy)

65. Primula (Primrose)

66. Iris pseudacorus (Yellow flag)

67. Plantago cornuti (Plantain)

68. Nigella arvensis (Relative of Love-in-a-mist)

TAPESTRY NO. 4
The Unicorn at Bay

Tapestry No. 4

69. Arbutus unedo (Strawberry tree)
70. Prunus armeniaca (Apricot)
71. Quercus robur (English oak)
72.   ?
73.   ?
74. Chrysanthemum parthenium (Feverfew)
75. Stratiotes aloides (Water-soldier)
76. Typha latifolia (Cattail)
77. Myosotis scorpiodes (Forget-me-not)
78.   ?
79. Cirsium arvense ("Canada" thistle)
80. Prunus persica (Peach)

Tapestry No. 5
The Mystic Hunt of the Unicorn (two fragments)

Tapestry No. 5

The right-hand fragment of these two contains the only apple tree shown in the entire series. It apparently formed the central feature of the original fifth tapestry, in which the unicorn has been captured by the Virgin. A huntsman and one of the Virgin's handmaidens are shown here, one without, the other within, the rose-entwined enclosure.

81. Malus pumila (Apple)

Tapestry No. 6

The Unicorn Is Killed and Brought to the Castle

Tapestry No. 6

82. Rubus fruticosus (Blackberry)
83. Iris germanica (Bearded iris)
84. Cucubalus baccifer
85. Phyllitis scolopendrium (Hart's-tongue fern)
86. Carthamus tinctorius (Safflower)
87.   ?

Tapestry No. 7

88.   ?
89. Scilla nonscripta (fruit) (English bluebell)
90. Senecio doronicum (Leopard's bane)
91. Mathiola incana (Stock)
92. Polygonum bistoria (Bistort)
93. Orchis mascula (Male orchid)
94. Dianthus caryophyllus (Carnation)
95. Arum maculatum (Cuckoo-pint, Lords and ladies)
96.   ?
97. Primula elatior (Oxlip)
98. Silybum marianum (Holy, Milk, or St. Mary's thistle)
99. Aquilegia vulgaris (Columbine)
100. Lilium candidum (Madonna lily)
101. Taraxacum officinale (Dandelion)

Tapestry No. 7
The Unicorn in Captivity

Appendix II: Fauna in the Unicorn Tapestries

The following is an abridged version of Chapter 3 in "The Birds and Beasts of the Tapestries," from Margaret L. Freeman's The Unicorn Tapestries (New York, 1976), pp. 67–90. The tapestries are discussed in the order in which the author believed they belonged.

The unicorn is the hero of the Cloisters' tapestries, but other animals and birds play significant roles in the story. All of them, unlike the unicorn, are real, though obviously not all were familiar to the artist who designed the tapestries. Many of them are included in the bestiaries, where their habits are described with little regard for the true facts but a great deal of concern for "much moral teaching."

The Unicorn is Found [Figure 34]

Gathered at the stream where the unicorn dips his horn are a lion and lioness, stag, panther, genet, and hyena. A rabbit sits near the fountain, and another, perhaps tired of waiting for the stream to be purified, retreats into its hiding place. A pair of pheasants perch on the fountain's rim, the male observing his reflection in the water. Two European goldfinches have flown to the edge of the fountain, and what is probably a nightingale rests on a bush nearby. All of these creatures had symbolic meanings to the medieval mind.

THE LION

The poet Philippe de Thaun wrote in his bestiary (about 1121): "The lion in many ways rules over many beasts, therefore is the lion king. . . . The lion signifies the son of St. Mary; he is king of all the people."

The bestiaries further note three "natures" of the lion that make him a symbol of Christ. According to Bishop Theobald (probably eleventh century) and his medieval commentator:

The first characteristic is that he dwells in the highest mountains . . . and however long the way may be for him, he descends . . . to the valley, and if by chance he should perceive a hunter, at once with his tail he rubs out the marks of his feet lest by them, the hunter should find his den. . . . As the lion dwells on

the high mountain, so Christ, the spiritual lion, dwells in the highest heaven. . . . And as the lion when he comes down from the mountain wipes out with his tail the marks of his feet . . . so Christ when He descended from heaven into the womb of the glorious Virgin Mary in order that He might redeem the human race by his Incarnation, hid himself so that not one of the Demons knew Christ to be the Son of God. . . .

The second characteristic of the lion is that he produces his offspring without life . . . until the third day of its birth, and then the father of the young thing . . . sends forth a great roar . . . and thus arouses it as if from sleep. . . . This second characteristic of the lion is thus compared to Christ . . . [who] himself lay dead in the sepulcher until the third day, and on the third day God the Father aroused him by such a voice as this: "Awake up my glory, awake lute and harp."

The lion bringing to life his cubs, born dead, was a popular allegory of the Resurrection. Even some theologians accepted this strange "nature" of the lion as true. Honorius of Autun, in the twelfth century, made use of it in his sermon for Easter Sunday, and the great Peter Abelard (1079–1142) writes: "As the young of the lion, so Our Lord is risen . . . on the third day."

The third characteristic of the lion, according to Bishop Theobald, is that "whenever he sleeps, his eyelids never are closed." Theobald's commentator explains:

The lion is thus compared to Christ . . . for Christ never closes the eyes of his tender mercy, but always guards us as a watchful shepherd, lest the . . . Devil should carry off any one from His flock. The Psalmist saith . . . "Behold He that keepeth Israel shall neither slumber nor sleep."

Guillaume le Clerc gives further meaning to this nature of the lion, saying that when Christ "was set upon the Cross . . . his human self suffered death . . . but then his divinity was awake. . . . Man can wound the human form without harming the divine nature. . . ."

Another characteristic of the lion is that,

though he is monarch of all beasts, he is "harassed by the tiny sting of the scorpion, and snake poison kills him."

It is also written in the Cambridge bestiary that the lions' "courage is seated in their ears, while their constancy is in their heads." And it is further stated that the lion, "like the king he is, disdains to have a lot of different wives."

The lion was used by poets in other ways than as a symbol of love. Wolfram von Eschenbach (late twelfth to thirteenth century), in his *Parzifal,* likens his hero and half-brother to two lion's whelps because they were roused to life and activity by the roar of battle. And a wandering scholar in the thirteenth century admonished the rulers of the church and state to take example from the lion. . . .

The lion is indeed an animal worthy to associate with the unicorn. He too is a symbol of Christ; he too is courageous and merciful; he too stands for fidelity in love. . . . He is included in almost every group of animals being created by God or named by Adam or waiting to go aboard Noah's ark. Further, he appears without accompanying animals in countless medieval representations, for he was a favorite medieval beast.

THE STAG

According to the twelfth-century bestiary of Philippe de Thaun:

> The stag has that nature . . . that he goes seeking a hole where there is a serpent lying. When he has found a serpent, he takes water in his mouth and throws it in and then blows. He blows there . . . so long that he draws [the serpent] out with great labor. The stag is angry and kills it with his feet. . . . By this stag we rightly understand Jesus Christ. The water is wisdom which is in his mouth; . . . holy inspiration is understood by his blowing, and by the serpent, the Devil.

The bestiary of Bishop Theobald says that the stag, instead of stomping on the serpents, devours them, and "soon by the strength of their poison is heated." He "hastens then to the spring, knowing its waters are cool. Here he greedily drinks, and the poison is quenched by the water." By this

means, too, "he makes himself young, at which time he casts off his horns." Thus men, when they gather poisons from the serpent, such as "luxury, hatred, anger . . . [or] lusts of the heart . . . should run with all haste to Christ, who is our living water, who when he cleanses our souls, drives all poison away. Now, if our sins are thus cleansed, we are once again youthful and happy."

A second characteristic of the stag as told in the Cambridge bestiary is

> that when they change their feeding grounds for love of a foreign pasture . . . if by any chance they have to cross huge rivers or seas, each rests his head on the haunches of the one in front, and, since the one behind does the same thing for him in turn, they suffer no trouble from the weight. And . . . they hurry across with the greatest possible speed for fear of getting befouled. [Thus] when Christians leave their pasture, i.e., their world, for the love of heavenly pastures, they support each other, i.e., the more perfect carry along and sustain the weight of the less perfect by their example and good works. And if they come across some occasion for sin they hurry over it at once.

Other traits and habits of stags that are not fitted laboriously with morals are described in several of the bestiaries. According to the Cambridge manuscript, they "listen admiringly to the music of rustic pipes," which they hear well when their ears are up, though when their ears are lowered they hear nothing at all. In the mating season, "the males . . . bell with the fury of concupiscence." The females "do not conceive until the time of the star Arcturus, nor do they bring forth their babies just anywhere, but they hide them with tender care, and, having tucked them up in some deep shrubbery . . . they admonish them with a stamp of the foot to keep hidden."

When stags hear the cry of hounds, they "place themselves with a following wind, so that their scent may blow away. . . . All stand stock still, for which reason they make themselves an easier mark for archers." But "they can shake off any arrows which they may have received" if they partake of the herb called dittany.

The horns of the stag are of value to man.

"The one . . . which is on the right of the head is the more useful . . . for healing things. To keep snakes away, you can burn either of them." Also, "It is known that stags never get feverish, so, for this reason, ointments made from their marrow will settle heats in sick men." And "many people who have been accustomed to eat venison from their early days have been immortal, and immune to fevers, but it fails them in the end if they happen to get killed by a single wound."

In certain love caskets and tapestries, the hunt of the stag becomes an allegory of the search for faithfulness in love. Pursuing a stag, the huntsman-lover on the lid of a Minnekästchen [love casket] of about 1400 urges on his hounds with the words: "Run with all speed, for Faithfulness will go into the forest." Between the antlers of the stag are two clasped hands, symbol of trust and fidelity.

On the front of another Minnekästchen two deer are collared and roped to miniature trees. On the back of this box two confronting unicorns wear collars also, with rings for attaching leashes or chains. It is regrettable that there are no scrolls with inscriptions here. . . . Although the inscriptions are frequently difficult to decipher and translate, the words at least give clues to the meaning of the scene. In any case, it seems evident that a parallel is intended here between the unicorns and the deer. It also seems evident that the noble stag of the Cloisters' tapestry is present at the water-purification scene because he was a familiar beast of the forest and a favorite animal of the chase and also because he symbolized by his "natures" some of the finest qualities of man.

THE PANTHER

The modern zoologist says that the spotted animal in the foreground of [*The Unicorn Is Found*] should be termed a leopard, and the modern encyclopedist states that the panther is in truth a leopard, but the modern medievalist prefers to call him a panther, since in medieval literature, he is usually referred to as a *pantera* (Latin or a *panthère* [French]).

According to the bestiaries, the panther is exceedingly beautiful. Bishop Theobald describes him as "having a coat which is white but sprinkled with numberless round spots." Another source says that he is "many-colored like the coat of Joseph . . . and adorned like a queen." Guillaume le Clerc is specific about the many colors: he is "white and light blue and dark, and yellow and green and russet-brown." Moreover, the panther is good-tempered, gentle, and intelligent; and he is loved by all the animals except the dragon alone.

He has "this nature: . . . when he has eaten and is filled, he sleeps in his den. And the third day he arises from sleep, crying out with a loud voice. And the animals that are nigh and that are afar off hear his voice. From his voice there streams all the fragrance of spices. And the animals follow the fragrance of the panther's smell, running up to it." Only the dragon flees.

The panther, as might be expected, is interpreted in the bestiaries as another symbol of Christ. He is beautiful, and so is Christ. He is many-colored; and Christ also is "manifold . . . since he is virginity, temperance, compassionateness, faith, virtue, patience, concord, peace." And "when Christ was roused on the third day and rose from the dead, all fragrance came to us, both the peaceable ones that are nigh and those that are afar off." As Guillaume le Clerc wrote:

> Of the beast which is so sweet
> We have again a lesson ready;
> For sweetness is an attribute of God. . . .
> More sweet are his commandments
> Than sweet spices and ointments.
> If we do his commandments
> Rich will be the reward.
> God will set us in his palace
> In the beautiful city of peace,
> In the heavenly Jerusalem,
> On the high hill, where it is so good to be,
> Where no one will be sad.

It is not surprising that the panther, because of his beauty, his good temper, and his sweetness, was taken over by the troubadours and other romantic writers as a symbol of the beloved. Richard de Fournival tells his beloved that, captivated by her sweetness, he has abandoned his own wishes to follow hers, "just as the animals, after they have once scented the sweet odor of the panther, never afterward will they leave her, but follow her until death." Fournival's panther, as in other love allegories, is appropriately of the feminine gender.

The love allegory is developed at greater length in the poem "La Panthère d'Amours," written by Nicole de Margival at the end of the thirteenth or beginning of the fourteenth century. Here again the beloved, to whom Nicole addresses his work, is symbolized by the panther. The poet dreams that he is carried off to a forest where he sees lions, stags, "unicorns and other beasts with horns." There he is struck by the beauty of one beast that all the animals love except the dragon only. While he watches in admiration the beautiful animal disappears. Then the God of Love arrives to the sound of music, and, together, the poet and the god go in search of the marvelous creature. Finally he perceives her at some distance hidden in a hollow at the foot of a valley surrounded by a hedge of blackberries and thistles. The god explains the hidden sense of what he has just seen: ". . . the beast that is so beautiful and so noble" is the panther, and it signifies the lady toward whom the poet directs all his thoughts and his wishes for love. The many colors of the beast symbolize the abundance of virtues and graces that the lady possesses. The good sweet breath of the panther cures all ills, and that is why the animals follow her; the lady, like the panther, heals all vices such as "pride" and "outrage" in those who surround her "in her own country." The dragon represents the envious and the covetous. The valley to which the panther has retired "signifies humility," the blackberries and thistles represent "amorous thoughts," but the thorns symbolize the "cruel attacks of slanderers.". . .

It is fortunate that the panther of the Cloisters' tapestry is more accurately represented than, for instance, the panther in Fournival's *Bestiaire d'Amours*; otherwise, without accompanying text for guidance, the animal in the manuscript could not have been identified. And this would have been a pity, for the panther, by the richness of its symbolism, both religious and secular, adds considerably to the meaningful group of animals assembled by the stream with the unicorn.

THE GENET, WEASEL, AND ERMINE
To the right of the panther is a genet, an animal not often found in the bestiaries. It may be that the artist who designed the tapestry liked the genet, delighting in its long, lithe body and elegantly ringed tail, and perhaps assigned to it some of the symbolism of the *Mustela*, or weasel, an animal that, to the unscientific eye, resembles the genet and figures importantly in the books of beasts.

The "great marvel" of the weasel, according to Guillaume le Clerc and others, is that "she receives by mouth the seed whereby she conceives," and "by the ear brings forth" her young. "Some say," however, that weasels "conceive through the ear and give birth through the mouth." After the weasel "has had her babies . . . she moves [them] from place to place with subtle cunning . . . and always lies at night in a different lair." According to a French herbal printed about 1500, the *Ortus Sanitatis*, the weasel is "so skilled in medicine that if she should find her babies dead, she can make them come alive again with a certain herb that she knows."

Weasels hunt mice and snakes, and, according to Bartholomaeus Anglicus, the basilisk; this "king of serpents," in whose "sight no fowl nor bird passeth harmless . . . is overcome by the weasel. . . . For the Father and Maker of everything left nothing without a remedy." The weasel is "small in body . . . but large in subtlety, and in courage." The moral teaching to be learned from the weasel, according to the bestiaries, is derived from the "great marvel" that impregnation is effected through one orifice while birth takes place through another. In the words of the Cambridge bestiary: "These creatures signify not a few of you fellows, who willingly accept by ear the seed of God's word, but who, shackled by the love of earthly things, put it away in the wrong place and dissimulate what you hear."

A species of *Mustela* that turns white in winter is the ermine. Because of its whiteness, no doubt, it was a popular symbol of chastity. In the triumphal procession of Chastity, as described by Petrarch, "the banner of victory displayed an ermine, white upon a field of green wearing a chain of topaz and of gold." In the Marietta print [see Figure 24], where the maiden is about to enchain a unicorn, a collared ermine at the feet of the lady bears witness to her purity.

If indeed the Cloisters' genet is intended to be equated with the weasel, possessing the weasel's virtues as explained in the books of beasts, it is in the company of its peers. It has great courage, as has the lion. It is solicitous of its young, as are the lion and the deer. It is the enemy of serpents, as are the stag, panther, and unicorn. If, after all, the designer considered the animal only as a genet, it is at least an attractive addition to the group of beasts at the stream. It turns its head in surprise at the ugly creature who has joined the company. This creature is the hyena.

THE HYENA

There is little to be said in favor of the hyena. According to the bestiaries it lives in the sepulchers of the dead and devours their bodies. It imitates the voices of shepherds, and by this ruse calls out men and dogs at night to their harm. "Its nature is that at one moment it is masculine and at another feminine, and hence it is a dirty brute."

The moral lessons to be learned from the changeable nature of the hyena are explained by Guillaume le Clerc:

> This beast, doubt it not,
> Denotes the children of Israel,
> Who at first firmly believed
> In the true Father omnipotent
> And held to him loyally
> But afterwards became as females.
> When they partook of delicate foods
> And gave themselves to pleasures,
> To the flesh and to luxury
> No more did they regard the lord God,
> But forsook him and were so foolish
> That they worshiped idols. . . .
> Many are the folk, it seemeth to me,
> Who are like to this beast . . .
> Double-minded and weak and lying,
> Nor in any way are they stable.
> Of these is the word of Solomon
> Who made the book of sermons:
> A double-minded man, false and dissembling,
> Who at no time is constant
> In anything which he does or says,
> His is a very evil life.

The least unpleasant characteristic of the hyena is that it has in its eye a precious gem, and:

> Whoever under his tongue should keep it
> They say that he should foretell
> Things which are to happen
> In the events of this world.

The French *Ortus Sanitatis* states that the hyena can even be of physical benefit to man: "The spleen of this animal restores clearness to the eyes, the dung heals infected wounds, and the hair from its head cures the headache."

The presence of the hyena in the tapestry along with the "good" animals is not as strange as it may seem, for medieval artists frequently depicted creatures that symbolized the Devil and wickedness in man adjacent to those that symbolized God and man's better natures. They apparently enjoyed the contrast that resulted. Guillaume le Clerc rationalizes the inclusion of the hyena in his bestiary thus:

> . . . it teaches
> In what form evil still exists
> And the way which he should go
> Who wills to return to God.

THE RABBITS

The French *Ortus Sanitatis* states that rabbits "give birth many times a year," have "little ones without number," and "multiply marvelously."

Rabbits are conspicuous in all six of the *Lady with the Unicorn* tapestries in the Musée de Cluny (see Figures 69–74). They appear also in many other medieval works of art, not necessarily because of their significance but because of their undeniable charm.

THE DOGS

Dogs appear in six of the unicorn tapestries as essentials of the hunt. . . . Here it will not be out of place to pay tribute to them, as do the books of beasts, for their intelligence and their devotion to their masters. Says the writer of the Cambridge bestiary:

> Now none is more sagacious than the Dog, for he has more perception than other animals and he alone recognizes his own name. He esteems his Master highly. There are numerous

breeds of dogs. Some track down the wild creatures of the woods. . . . Others guard the flocks of sheep vigilantly against infestations of wolves. Others, the house-dogs, look after the palisade of their masters, lest it should be robbed in the night by thieves, and these will stand up for their owners to the death.

In the Middle Ages the dog, more than any other animal, symbolized fidelity.

THE PHEASANT

The pheasant observing his reflection in the mirrorlike surface of the fountain with his mate beside him is indeed, as the French *Ortus Sanitatis* says, "a very beautiful bird." His "plumage is resplendent in the manner of fire . . . blue and green and shining bright with feathers of a red color." Moreover he is "courageous and bold," but "he is sad when it rains." The male and female "live together only in times of love, and at all other times they are separated."

The *Livre de chasse du roy Modus* (before 1377) describes how the pheasant may be trapped by placing a large mirror in a cage. When he sees himself in the mirror and thinks that it is another bird, he strikes against the mirror and is thus caught. It seems that "the pheasant cannot abide another male pheasant near him . . . for he is never without his mate and he is jealous of his own reflection . . . believing that he is seeing a rival."

It is possible that the exquisitely woven reflection of the pheasant in the fountain was suggested by the account in the *Livre de chasse* of the pheasant beholding himself in a mirror. In any case, the reflection probably recalls the symbolic "unblemished mirror" of secular and religious symbolism. In the *Romance of the Rose*, that great medieval love allegory, the mirror in which the lover sees his beloved rose is in the fountain of the Garden of Delight.

In the Middle Ages the pheasant, a noble bird, was associated with the nobility. Duke Philip the Good of Burgundy held a sumptuous feast at Lille in 1454, on which occasion a live pheasant with a jeweled collar was brought before him. In the presence of all his courtiers, the duke swore "before

God . . . the Glorious Virgin Mary . . . and the Pheasant" that, unless illness prevented, "he would follow the king of France to free the Holy Land." The feast has since been known as the Feast of the Pheasant. . . .

THE EUROPEAN GOLDFINCH

Two European goldfinches are placed conspicuously in the center of [*The Unicorn Is Found*], an adult bird standing motionless on the rim of the fountain, a fledgling fluttering its wings beside it.

The goldfinch "feeds on thorns and thistles," according to Isidore of Seville and others. Albertus Magnus says, more sensibly, that it "eats the seeds of thorns and thistles." In the Middle Ages almost any prickly plant could be identified with Christ's crown of thorns and so could be considered holy. Accordingly, through its association with thistles and thorns, the goldfinch is related to Christ's Passion and man's redemption. Konrad von Megenburg writes:

It is a great wonder that the bird sings so beautifully although it feeds on the sharp spines of the thistle. It is thus a symbol of the good preacher on earth who has to endure greatly, yet even among the thorns of this world joyfully serves God. O, God . . . thou art well acquainted with meals of thorns; yet Thou too has sung on earth unto the bitter death.

Besides the goldfinches on the fountain, another perches at the left on a small medlar, a thorny tree related to the rose. In [*The Unicorn Leaps out of the Stream*], and also in [*The Unicorn at Bay*], a goldfinch flies into the sky from a clump of trees in which the holly is conspicuous. In [*The Unicorn Is Killed and Brought to the Castle*] two goldfinches appear in a spiny hawthorn immediately behind the dead unicorn as he is brought to the lord and lady of the castle.

A great many devotional paintings depict the goldfinch, most often held by the Christ child, as in a painting by Carlo Crivelli, about 1480, in the Metropolitan Museum. Even if the goldfinch had lacked symbolic significance, the designer of the tapestries might have included it among the fauna of the forest, for it was (and is) an elegant little bird with its black hood, ruby red throat, and wings streaked with brilliant yellow. It was well loved throughout Europe in the Middle Ages, whether flying free or living in a cage as a household pet.

It is perhaps significant that an adult bird is accompanied by a young one in [*The Unicorn Is Found*]. According to Pliny, the goldfinch, though a small bird, produces a dozen little ones, whereas large animals like the elephant, camel, and horse, produce but one. The goldfinch thus became another symbol of fecundity.

THE NIGHTINGALE

The inconspicuous bird poised on a bush above the fountain at the left is probably a nightingale. The eighth-century scholar Alcuin, in a poem for his lost nightingale, writes:

So brown and dim that little body was,
  But none could scorn thy singing. In that
  throat,
That tiny throat, what depth of harmony,
  And all night long ringing thy changing note.
  What marvel if the cherubim in heaven
Continually do praise Him, when to thee,
  O small and happy, such a grace was given?

The Cambridge bestiary says that the nightingale is

accustomed to herald the dawn of a new day with her song. . . . She is an ever-watchful guardian, too, for she warms her eggs with a certain hollow of the body and with her breast. She tempers the sleepless labour of her long night's work by the sweetness of her song. . . . In imitation of this bird, the poor but honest working woman, as she toils . . . so that a subsistence of bread may not be lacking for her babies, yet lightens the burden of poverty by her nightly song, and however unable she may be to imitate the lovely measures of the nightingale, yet she does imitate it nevertheless by the diligence of her devotion.

However, the nightingale's long association with springtime, the burgeoning earth, and lovers seems even more pertinent—and more delightful. The French *Ortus Sanitatis* explains that the name

Filomena for nightingale originated in two Greek words meaning "sweet" and "love." Medieval poets over and over again introduce the nightingale into their love lyrics, as did a wandering scholar of the thirteenth century:

O Nightingale, be still
  For an hour,
Till the heart sings:
  With the love of a maid
Aflower,
  With the love of a maid
Afire,
  New love, new love,
Dying of desire.

The Unicorn Leaps out of the Stream [Figure 39]

Here, where the unicorn leaps the rushing brook, a mallard duck flies toward the water, a domestic white duck settles upon it, and a rusty-breasted bittern swims peacefully along. As far as can be determined, these birds are not symbolic. It is possible, however, that the pair of bright-eyed partridges partially hidden by blossoming plants at the water's edge were intended to convey some particular message.

THE PARTRIDGE

The books of beasts have much to say concerning this game bird, notably that it is often a thief. According to Philippe de Thaun, "When it sees the eggs of another, if it can it will steal them, it will put them in its own nest, then it will sit on them, and will breed them until they can eat well, fly, and produce eggs." But then if the chicks hear the voice of their true father or mother, "they will desert those who have bred them" and go to their real kin, "therefore nature is more powerful than breeding." The "signification" is that the "partridge which is wicked . . . is the Devil . . . who takes from the Holy Church that which it had baptized." But "when these Christian people . . . hear the voice of God and of the Holy Church, they desert the Devil . . . who then looks upon himself as disgraced." It may be noted in defense of partridges that apparently not all of them steal eggs and thus not all are evil.

The bestiaries say further that the partridge is very astute. In the words of the Cambridge bestiary:

> if a man comes near the place where a partridge is brooding, the mother . . . shows herself of her own accord, and feigning feebleness of foot and wing as if she might be caught at any moment, invents all sorts of ways to hasten slowly away. By this stratagem she entices and deludes the passer-by until he is coaxed away from the nest. . . . So you see that they are not slow in employing zeal to guard their babies.

Also:

> Partridges secure protective coloration by clever camouflage. They cover their setts with thorny shrubs, so that animals which might attack them are kept off by the sharpness of the twigs. Dust is used as a covering for the eggs, and the birds return to the nest circuitously. . . . When partridges notice that they have been spied out, they turn over on their backs, lift clods of earth with their feet, and spread these so skillfully to cover themselves that they lie hidden from detection.

According to the bestiaries, partridges are by nature "lustful" and have "great desire to cohabit," the cocks fight furiously for their hens, and so fertile is the female that "even if a wind blows toward them from the males they become pregnant."

The designer of the tapestries may or may not have had in mind any of these characteristics of the partridge when he included a pair of them, plump-breasted and quietly watchful, in the tapestry where the hunters give full chase to the fleeing unicorn.

The Unicorn at Bay [Figure 44]

THE HERON

In the tumultuous tapestry where huntsmen thrust their spears, the unicorn gores a hound, and woodcocks and mallards flutter about, one creature alone seems unperturbed. This is the heron at the lower right, standing on one leg near a peach tree, stately, oblivious to the fray, and magnificently serene. The heron is known for its lofty flight. According to Isidore of Seville and others, it "fears the rainstorms and so it flies above the clouds in order to avoid the tempests. Thus, when it soars to great heights it is a sign of bad weather."

Hrabanus Maurus (about 776–856) explains that "this bird signifies the souls of the elect," who, fearing the tempests of persecutions instigated by the devil, fly above all frightening temporary events to the serenity of heaven where they may behold forever the countenance of God."

Pseudo-Hugo of St. Victor says that the "heron seeks its food in the water, but it builds its nest in the high trees." They defend their young fiercely with their beaks lest they be carried from their nests by other birds.

The heron was one of the "noble birds" on which medieval knights ceremoniously took their vows to embark on dangerous and noble ventures.

The Unicorn Is Killed and Brought to the Castle [Figure 50]

Here a turreted castle is featured, complete with dovecote and a moat in which swans are swimming. It is probable that the doves and the swans were included chiefly because, in the Middle Ages, they were a normal part of castle life. However, it may be that the designer also had in mind some of the observations on these birds in the books of beasts.

THE SWAN

The Cambridge bestiary says that the swan "pours out a sweetness of music with melodious note" and "the reason why this bird sings so beautifully is because it has a long, curved neck" and the rich music "goes round and round through the lengthy bend." It also says that in northern parts of the world, when "the lute players have tuned up, a great many swans are invited in, and they play a concert together in strict measure." The swan, says this same book, "is a fowl most cheerful in auguries," and sailors "quite rightly say that this bird brings good luck."

Bartholomaeus Anglicus adds: "When the

swan is in love he seeketh the female and pleaseth her with clipping of the neck, and draweth her to him . . . and he joineth his neck to the female's neck, as it were binding the necks together."

THE DOVE

"The Dove is a simple fowl and free from gall, and it asks for love with its eye," according to the Cambridge bestiary. "Among all the other birds, the dove is a courtly and pretty one and has good meaning," writes Guillaume le Clerc. "The Holy Spirit in the likeness of it descended at the baptizing of Jesus Christ. And . . . many a time it has happened that in its likeness, has come the Holy Spirit for to comfort those whom man is wont to persecute."

Philippe de Thaun, quoting Isidore of Seville, says: "There is a dove that makes others come to its dovecote; and when they are assembled, they all have their wishes; of various colors are the doves that go there. . . . The dove signifies Jesus the Son of Mary, and we are his doves."

The kind of dove known as turtur or turtledove has this characteristic: it will mate but once in its life. In the words of the Cambridge bestiary: "It is truly believed that when a turtledove is widowed by the loss of her spouse, she takes a dread against the marriage bed and against the very name of matrimony." She does not "break the bonds of chastity or forget the rights of her wedded husband. She keeps her love for him alone, for him she guards the name of wife."

THE SQUIRREL

In a hazelnut tree in the lower left corner of this tapestry sits a red squirrel with sharp tufted ears, beady eyes, and bushy tail curved over its back. He seems intent on smelling one of the tree's blossoms.

Vincent of Beauvais describes the squirrel as a "small animal larger than a weasel . . . elegant and beautiful to see. . . . It lives in trees and has its young there. . . . Men and women take pride in ornamenting their garments with skins; but the little animal itself does not glory in its own fur nor in that of others."

The French *Ortus Sanitatis* adds that it has a

"marvelous lightness" and when it "jumps from tree to tree it sometimes uses its tail for wings." And if it needs to "pass over a body of water in the woods in a sort of small boat" it raises its tail as if it were a sail and the wind blows it across. "It gathers its food in the summer and lives on it in the winter."

An unidentified source, probably medieval, says that "when the squirrel is hunted she cannot be driven to the ground unless extremity of faintness causes her to do so . . . for such is the stately mind of this little beast that while her limbs and strength lasteth, she . . . saveth herself in the tops of tall trees . . . knowing, indeed, her greatest danger rests below amongst the dogs and busy hunters. From whence may be gathered, a perfect pattern for us, to be secured from all the evils and hungry chasings of the treacherous devil; namely that we keep above in the lofty palaces of heavenly meditations, for there is small security in this on earth."

The squirrel of this tapestry may be intended to be symbolic, or it may be present merely to call attention to the hazelnut tree in which it sits.

THE HORSE

A splendid horse appears in this tapestry, bearing the beautiful dead unicorn on his back to the lord and lady of the castle. In the Middle Ages horses were essential for knightly existence, and excellent ones were often valued above all other possessions, even wives. According to the Cambridge bestiary, a fine horse should have a powerful body, small head, "short and lively" ears, erect neck, dense mane and tail, and an "audacious" spirit. It should be "swift of foot and trembling in its limbs. The latter is an indication of courage. . . . God himself gives courage to the horse and unharnesses fear from his neck—so that he leaps about on the plains and is pleasing to kings as he gallops."

The Unicorn in Captivity [Figure 24]

In this tapestry three winged insects are conspicuous among the flowers: a butterfly hovers over the carnation that grows in front of the unicorn's enclosure, a dragonfly inspects the blue iris nearby, and another dragonfly touches the Madonna lily.

A small frog lies motionless, almost hidden among violets, above the A of the monogram in the tapestry's lower right-hand corner.

THE BUTTERFLY

The butterfly is believed to signify love and fertility. Also, since it evolved from a lower caterpillar to an exquisite winged creature, it may be intended to symbolize the resurrection of Christ and of man as well. So far, these interpretations have not been documented by medieval texts. Aristotle calls the butterfly the "psyche," meaning the soul.

THE FROG

Aelian and Bartholomaeus Anglicus write of the wooing and mating of the frog. According to Aelian, "the frog, as a signal that he wishes to mate, emits a certain cry to the female, like a lover singing a serenade, and this cry is called its croak, so they say."

Pliny claims that a bone from the left side of the frog, worn as an amulet, serves as an aphrodisiac. Aelian notes that the frog "abhors and greatly fears the water snake. Accordingly, in return it tries to terrify and scare the water snake by its loud croaking." According to several writers, Hildegard von Bingen among them, the frog may be used to heal cases of poisoning: "If a person has poison anywhere in his body, except the head, and is weakened, let him take a frog and strangle it over a small herb . . . and immediately place a warm bandage over the part of the body where the poison is raging, and at once place the dying frog on this bandage for just an hour, and the poisoning in that place will cease for a year or a year and a half."

Of these birds and beasts, the ones that were familiar to the designer and the weavers of the tapestries are remarkably lifelike. The birds fly freely or dip into the streams, not in the least entrapped by the warp and weft of the fabric. The pheasant is as resplendent as a pheasant should be. The squirrel could jump from twig to twig at any moment, and its fur seems softer than the wool of which it is woven.

The more exotic beasts—the lions and the panther—are less convincing. They were apparently not drawn from observation of the actual animals but instead from "pattern books" or manuscripts or paintings or prints available in the workshop. It is remarkable that the unicorn, the most exotic of them all, is truly the most full of life and the most reassuringly real.

These birds and beasts may be enjoyed today for their own sake, though medieval accounts of their "natures" and ways give them added dimension.

Suggestions for Further Reading

Shepard, Odell. *The Lore of the Unicorn* (Boston, 1930; reprinted 1979, 1982). Iconography and history of the unicorn discussed in great detail, with many illustrations.

Alexander, E. J., and Carol H. Woodward, "The Flora of the Unicorn Tapestries." *Journal of the New York Botanical Garden* (May–June 1941); reprinted as pamphlet 1941, 1947, 1965. Discussion of the flora in all seven tapestries, with diagrams showing the locations of trees and plants that had been identified up to that time. Reprinted in this volume.

Souchal, Geneviève. "Un grand peintre français de la fin du XVe siècle: Le maître de la Chasse à la Licorne." *Revue de l'art*, no. 22 (1973), pp. 22–49. Discussion of the artist to whom this author attributed the design of *The Hunt of the Unicorn*. Richly illustrated, especially with Parisian woodcuts of the period.

Freeman, Margaret B. *The Unicorn Tapestries* (New York, 1974). A brief, forty-eight-page picture book, originally published as a Museum *Bulletin*, describing the tapestries.

———. *The Unicorn Tapestries* (New York, 1976). The most comprehensive study ever made of the tapestries from every point of view; history of the unicorn; special notes on the flora and fauna and their symbolism and on the ciphers. Abundantly illustrated, including various related materials in other media and collections.

Williamson, John. *The Oak King, the Holly King, and the Unicorn: The Myths and Symbolism of the Unicorn Tapestries* (New York, 1986). Discussion of the symbolism in the tapestries from the point of view of a synthesis of pagan and Christian iconographies. Additional identification of the flora, with diagrams developed from Alexander and Woodward 1941. Illustrated.

Giblin, James Cross. *The Truth about Unicorns* (New York, 1991). History of the unicorn and how perceptions of it changed through the centuries. Many new data; illustrated.

Cavallo, Adolfo S. *Medieval Tapestries in The Metropolitan Museum of Art* (New York, 1993), pp. 297–327. Summary of earlier opinions concerning the tapestries along with the author's own opinions. Detailed discussion of technique in introduction; illustrated; extensive bibliography.

Erlande-Brandenburg, Alain. *La dame à la licorne* ([Paris], 1993). Complete and lucid discussion of the tapestries in Paris. Lavishly illustrated with colorplates and details of all six pieces in the set.